DO YOU THINK YOU'RE TOO OLD TO COMPETE FOR THAT JOB?

DO YOU FEEL TOO YOUNG TO WARRANT THAT PROMOTION?

DO YOU SEE YOURSELF AS TOO UNATTRACTIVE TO LAND THAT GUY?

If you do, then you're involved in a lot of negative thinking that can and should be corrected. After all, locked within you are the same powers that have existed in all the famous people of history—all you have to do is bring them up from inside.

SELF-HYPNOSIS: YOUR KEY TO SUCCESSFUL LIVING explains how this can be done with minimum effort and maximum effectiveness. By teaching you how to communicate with your subconscious and direct your unconscious, it allows you to realize your full creative potential. By showing you how to release your inhibitions and calm your nerves, it offers you future happiness you never dreamed possible. And by instructing you in the science of hypnosis itself, it guarantees you a richer, healthier, more satisfying life.

START SHAPING YOUR DESTINY NOW!
WITH
SELF-HYPNOSIS: YOUR KEY TO SUCCESSFUL LIVING

SELF-HYPNOSIS: YOUR KEY TO SUCCESSFUL LIVING

Terri Robbe
with Karl Schanzer

AWARD BOOKS
NEW YORK

TANDEM BOOKS
LONDON

FIRST AWARD PRINTING 1969

Copyright © 1969 by Terri Lee Robbe and Karl Schanzer

All rights reserved

AWARD BOOKS are published by
Universal Publishing and Distributing Corporation
235 East Forty-fifth Street, New York, N. Y. 10017

TANDEM BOOKS are published by
Universal-Tandem Publishing Company Limited
14 Gloucester Road, London SW7, England

Manufactured in the United States of America

CONTENTS

Foreword 9

Chapter I: TELL ME NO LIES. Your unseen twin—Negative conditioning—Uniting your two selves—Communicating with your subconscious—Commanding your subconscious—Positive conditioning 10

Chapter II: GETTING TO KNOW YOURSELF. Fear of the unknown—Habit patterns—Developing a balanced personality—A channel from conscious to subconscious—An exercise in remembering 14

Chapter III: SO I SAID TO MYSELF. The language of the subconscious—The pendulum method of communicating with the subconscious—Automatic writing—Discovering motives 18

Chapter IV: THROW AWAY YOUR CRUTCHES. Early learning—Risking failure—Emotion and destiny—Your motion picture screen—A picture of yourself 23

Chapter V: ALL THE WORLD'S A STAGE. External and internal self-images—Learning self-confidence—Daydreaming with a purpose—What role will you play?—How to play the leading role 26

Chapter VI: AND A LITTLE CHILD SHALL LEAD THEM. The child in yourself—The low self, the middle self, the high self—A diagram of the subconscious—A case history—Physical condition—Subconscious punishment 30

Chapter VII: THE PATH TO POWER. The power within yourself—The primitive approach—The natural order of things—Energy in the galaxy—Dissipating fears—Expressing the power to create 34

Chapter VIII: AN INNER MAGIC. Voodoo—Black Magic—White Magic—Having a focus—Having a formula—Believing—A case of hysterical paralysis—Confession can free the subconscious 37

Chapter IX: YOU *CAN* CONQUER PAIN. Martyrs and witches—Faith can prevent pain—The pain threshold—Short-circuiting pain—LSD and pain—The purpose of pain 43

Chapter X: THE PAIN WITHIN. Pain as a conditioner—Psychological pain—Eliminating mental pain—Preventing mental pain 48

Chapter XI: WORD MAGIC. The meaning of words—Ritual use of words—The power of words—Unintended word orders—Using the right words 53

Chapter XII: SUPERCHARGE YOUR OTHER SELF WITH LOVE. Using concepts constructively—Emotion as a force—Positive conditioning for your other self—Erasing negative emotion—The inner flow of divinity 58

Chapter XIII: ANY SUGGESTIONS? Suggestion rules destiny—The unconscious never sleeps—Conditioning through advertising—Making plants grow with faith—Concentrated suggestion—A breathing exercise 62

Chapter XIV: BELIEVE AND ACHIEVE. The reason for charisma—Physical charisma—Strengthening your charisma—Realizing expectations—A breathing exercise 67

Chapter XV: LONELINESS. Self-inflicted isolation—Feelings of rejection—Loneliness as a conditioned reflex—An exercise for relaxation—Giving love 71

Chapter XVI: SEX AND HAPPINESS. Procreation and pleasure—Confusion about sex—Some causes of frigidity—Sexual adequacy in men—Tracing the causes of the problem—Achieving sexual balance 75

Chapter XVII: DON'T WASTE YOUR TIME—LET YOUR KNOW-IT-ALL SUBCONSCIOUS DO THE WORK. Why do we sleep?—What happens without sleep?—Extra-sensory perception and sleep—Why do we dream?—Creativity and sleep—Solving problems during sleep 80

Chapter XVIII: OLD AGE—IT'S ALL IN YOUR MIND. Age and attitude—How to fight feeling futile—Rejuvenation drugs—The blueprint of yourself—The subconscious and aging—How to reverse the aging process 84

Chapter XIX: PARAPSYCHOLOGY—TOMORROW'S GIFT. Science and parapsychology—The existence of extra-sensory perception—Psychic power is in everyone—Uncontrolled psychic power 89

Chapter XX: NOBODY LIKES A BULLY. Mind and body—Exercising to build psychic balance—Commanding your whole being—Performing black magic—Misusing mental power ... 93

Chapter XXI: MYSTERIES OF THE FUTURE. Divination—Legendary seers—Methods of fortune telling—Drugs and divination—Contemporary fortune telling—Divination and the subconscious 97

Chapter XXII: THE MYSTERIES OF THE PAST. The accuracy of history—Interpretation of evidence—Discovering history psychically—The collective unconscious—Biological paths to history—Edgar Cayce's psychic investigations 103

Chapter XXIII: THE WORLD IN A CRYSTAL. Mirrors—Ink—Gems—Candle flames—How to use a crystal ball—How to coax the subconscious out—Crystal gazing can be destructive—Test your psychic powers 108

CHAPTER XXIV: DARK PATHS AND HIDDEN PITFALLS. Taking risks with power—How to recognize a "sensitive"—Exhaustion—Contact with the everyday world—The image-thinking society 114

Chapter XXV: THE VIOLENT INDIVIDUAL. Fundamentals of human behavior—Attitudes of populations—Survival—Fear—Violence and the law—The constructive power of anger 119

Chapter XXVI: THE GAP. Conflict between generations—Communication—Freeing subconscious convictions—Mutual exploitation—Who will win?—How to spread sanity 124

Chapter XXVII: TAKE FIVE . . . How to avoid being overwhelmed—Worry and energy—An example of obsessive behavior—The other self can take action—Fatigue—"Taking Five".. 130

Chapter XXVIII: RITE OF PASSAGE. Transitional ritual—Humanity will change—Fulfilling mankind's potential—Living in the present—People need people—Final advice............ 136

Foreword

These are times of change; mankind is on its way to other planets of our solar system. In a few years we'll be knocking at the doors of *real* space, looking across to the planets of other stars.

But people have a way of taking their troubles with them. No matter where our machines take us, frustration and lack of communication will make us miserable unless we learn to use the marvelous machinery of our minds.

This book is intended to lead you into paths as strange as any you would find in outer space; and in the depths of your own mind there may be creatures as strange as any in a science-fiction story. But while you may never land on Mars, you *must* learn to live with yourself—or suffer the consequences.

In many disguises, hypnosis has been used to guide the destinies of men since prehistoric times. No one knows exactly when it was first discovered that each human being has a subconscious mind, a separate person living in the same skull. But history is full of prophets and madmen who knew this, and knew how to control other people in ways that seemed ridiculous.

Self-hypnosis also has an honored place in history, but never under its own name. As a rule the techniques for mastering one's own hidden powers were closely guarded, passed on in hidden societies or given to disciples who were sworn to silence. Therefore one of the most important facts in human existence still has a flavor of the supernatural and is largely scorned for that reason.

But it is vital to understand this: *The part of you which really guides your destiny is not reading this page.* It lies in the back of your mind with most of its powers unused or devoted to hindering you, like a child who is naughty in an effort to be noticed.

Happiness lies in a whole personality. The authors have tried, in the simplest possible ways, to show how you can stop fighting yourself and achieve the happiness and success that you deserve . . .

Chapter I

TELL ME NO LIES

To most people, a large part of the human mind is as far away as the dark side of the moon—and, like any unknown land, it's full of mysteries, easier to ignore than explore. But since you're reading this book, you probably don't feel quite satisfied with your life. Maybe you're lonely or feel you're a failure. Maybe you're looking for something that will lift you out of the rut you've been in for years.

There's nothing in the world that can't be changed for the better. The answer to most of your problems is as close to you as your own shadow—and it's just as much a part of you. It lies on the other side of your conscious brain, in the unknown land where your subconscious mind lives.

Your subconscious is like a marvelous unseen twin, a brother or sister who has been with you since you were born, who shares your secrets and your dreams but can't talk to you about them. It is your other self.

Your other self regulates your physical and mental health. It handles your breathing, your heartbeat, all the necessary elements to keep you healthy—and you can use it to change these elements toward your improvement.

Your subconscious is where your memories are stored— and never lost. Everything that ever happened to you is permanently recorded just beyond the boundaries of your consciousness—and this can be good *or* bad.

As a child you learned there were many things you couldn't do. Parents and other adults taught you, as you grew up, that you had limits. Your other self preserved these lessons in failure, setting boundaries for you without conscious thought. Years later, you may have wondered why you gave up on something that mattered, when a little more energy or a different state of mind could have meant success.

You hold back your own abilities because you were taught to do so, and once the lesson was learned nothing you might do on the conscious level could change it because—consciously—you didn't know what was causing the problem.

You have to attack your negative beliefs on the subconscious level, where they were formed.

Your other self is both the keeper of your powers and the guard that keeps you from them. In spite of the forces it controls, it's a child, relying on you for the information on which it acts. Used correctly it can move the mountain of your own doubt. But in most modern, "civilized" people the subconscious mind is a mass of contradictions and half-truths, a tape-recorded history of *negative conditioning* which plays over and over again.

Negative conditioning is the result of false knowledge. As a child you absorbed a great many lies and misconceptions and learned to treat them as the truth. In later years, you gained a more accurate picture of reality and your conscious mind discarded the false beliefs of childhood. But your subconscious mind—the child within you —retained them.

At this point you're using a small fraction of your physical and mental powers. In fact, you're cut off from them by pressure, tension, worry—heavy chains of fear and doubt which were formed within you by yourself. Only you can break these chains, but you'll never use all your abilities unless you do. Trying to use the full potential of your mind with your subconscious bound up in negative attitudes is like trying to climb a mountain with an anchor on your back.

Remember that your other self is a twin part of *you,* with its own desires and frustrations. Yet it would be wrong to think of it as another personality. Instead you must realize that at this moment you're not a whole human being. When you and your other self are united, you'll be a whole person.

Right now, your subconscious is confused and resentful, lost in a mass of conflicting falsehoods and truths. It can only appeal to you: *"Tell me no lies!"* If you can truly communicate and wipe away the false information that's holding you back, you'll become—literally—a new human being.

Even in its present thwarted state, your other self is capable of working with you in small ways. Almost everyone, for instance, has used the subconscious as an "automatic alarm clock." If you haven't, try it. The next time you go to sleep, tell yourself to wake up at a particular time. Look at your clock, tell yourself strongly when you want to wake up—and you'll awaken at that moment. Your subconscious will keep track of the time for you while you sleep. You see, there's already *some* communication.

Without knowing it, you constantly send a stream of messages to your subconscious mind. But then, when your other self obeys your orders, you don't know why you feel the way you do. Your state of mind depends on the positive or negative directions you impress on yourself. You must be *consciously* aware that your other self is acting on your own commands.

Positive commands are those of success, confidence, power, love, health, creativity. If you impress your other self with these orders, you'll establish a cycle that will maintain itself.

Between positive and negative is a neutral area, a "gray" mental condition. In this state you're like a ship without a rudder, drifting helplessly at the whim of every mental breeze. Naturally it's easy to slip into negativity.

The negative state is dominated by feelings of failure, uselessness, poverty, fear, unhappiness in general. Like the positive side it will maintain itself once it starts, unless *you* do something to change it—and to change it, you must be able to break your negative conditioning.

During mankind's search for knowledge, many different ways have been found to break the chains of fear, to wake the sleeping giant in the minds of men. Some of these ways were once called magic. Almost all of them have names which are misleading, for the methods, like the problems, are basic and simple. You were conditioned to be a prisoner—and you must recondition yourself to be free.

Your goal lies far beyond easier communication with your subconscious, but this will be the first step in your program of *positive* conditioning: The ability to speak directly to your other self and to recognize its plea for understanding what you really wish to achieve.

Points to Remember from Chapter I

1. There's nothing in the world that can't be changed for the better.
2. Your other self—your subconscious mind—is the guardian of your unused powers.
3. Your failure in the past to use your full powers is the result of negative conditioning.
4. At this point you are not a complete human being. To be complete, you must unite your conscious and subconscious minds.
5. Your goal—positive reconditioning—lies with communication to and release of your other self.

Chapter II

GETTING TO KNOW YOURSELF

One reason why many people refuse to recognize the other self is fear of the unknown. It's true that some who enter the dark land of the subconscious become confused and lost, unable to find their way back—and being lost in such a place is a fearsome thing. But denying your other self will do nothing to make it vanish, and most frustrations and conflicts in our society arise when people won't recognize the subconscious as part of the whole human being.

Not only must you admit that your other self exists, but you must learn to know yourself—honestly. Naturally, since your subconscious is part of you, it shares all your past experiences, but it may not share your conscious likes and dislikes. Habit patterns you may have "outgrown" long ago are still cherished by the part of you that never forgot them. A childhood lesson may be faultily guiding an adult life.

Your subconscious is like a computer in its ability to help you. It will carry out *all* strongly directed orders from you, and often it has no way to distinguish between what's good or bad—it can only communicate a feeling of "wrongness," which it transmits by making you uncomfortable, or a feeling of "rightness," when it lets you feel wonderful, "for no reason." In harmony with it, you're strong—in conflict, you're weak. And no one can come out a winner when he fights himself.

Hold out both your hands in front of you and clasp them. Now push them against each other. You can push harder and harder—totally exhausting yourself—without accomplishing a thing. But working together your hands can build, make music, paint pictures. Your conscious and subconscious should be like your right and left hands, working together to create a balanced personality.

Since your other self follows your orders without thinking, you must be very careful what you give it in the way of information. For one thing, you must learn not to underestimate yourself. If you have a low opinion of your own abilities, that's just because you aren't aware of what you can do. But your other self will take you at your own value and *see to it* that you follow the limits you've set.

On the other hand, if you're convinced that you can handle anything the world tosses at you—that you're the match for whatever life offers—you will be!

Let's examine ways to form a channel from your conscious to your subconscious mind, so that your other self will understand your wishes clearly and simply. For this, relaxation and freedom from mental stress are necessary, so we'll use a method of suggestion loosely called self-hypnosis.

All types of conditioning, whether used on yourself or others, are forms of hypnosis. A politician who can sway crowds with his oratory and a man who finally decides he can diet in spite of his hunger are both using suggestion; both are calling on the powers in their subconscious minds to do it. Hypnosis is conditioning, and self-hypnosis is the easiest way through the forest of fear to your other self.

Start out with a very simple exercise. The next time you have a few minutes to spare—maybe just before you go to sleep—lie back and let your mind wander. Don't try to keep your mind blank, just relax and let the thoughts run through your head without trying to stop and examine them.

Naturally, first you'll think of things that have been happening recently. Let them pass, even if you'd like to stop and worry about your latest problems. When your mind finds that you don't want these thoughts right now, it will take them away.

After a while—like the surface of a lake growing calm when the ripples caused by wind fade away—your thoughts will grow more quiet, stop racing across the edge of your consciousness. Then you'll begin to notice little thoughts, recent memories that have been hanging around the corners of your mind, too small or unimportant to speak up and make themselves known.

Finally, your mind will become completely calm and you'll begin to remember things you haven't thought of for years. These memories will be startlingly clear, uncluttered by day-to-day worries and plans.

When you get this far—and you may not, the first time—try thinking of an experience you want to remember. Gently ask your other self for the particular memory. Then forget about it and relax. Don't rush the memory and don't worry if it doesn't arrive right away—there may be a lot of old files to look through.

Eventually, the recollection you want will come creeping into your mind, a little ragged around the edges at first, then clearer and clearer. If you want, you can live the whole experience over again—you'll even notice things you may not have seen the first time around. The important thing is to relax as this is happening; don't let the experience make you tense.

Don't be disappointed if the recollection isn't as vivid as you would like the first time. You *will* get better at it as you try again. Above all, reward your other self when the experience is over. You don't have to say anything out loud, but be happy—allow yourself a glow of satisfaction and achievement. Let your other self know when it does what you want and you'll get results fast.

This is the simplest form of conditioning. Later on you'll be meeting your other self "face to face," but for now it's enough to become friendly. It's a good step in the right direction, because you're beginning to use your whole mind and develop it fully—you're getting to know yourself!

Points to Remember from Chapter II

1. Most mental conflicts in our society are the result of a refusal to recognize the subconscious mind as part of the whole human being.
2. No one who uses only the conscious mind can develop to the fullest extent.
3. The subconscious mind is like a computer—it can only operate on the information you give it.
4. Self-hypnosis is a simple way to break down the wall between the conscious and the subconscious.
5. Let your first step be a short one—you must become acquainted with yourself.

Chapter III

SO I SAID TO MYSELF...

Almost everyone, these days, knows a few facts about the subconscious. It has become fashionable to talk about subconscious desires or feelings. Yet, to most people, the subconscious is a vague concept, existing in others but not in themselves.

Maybe it's too disturbing to admit that within *you* is another thinking creature, part of yourself but only able to communicate in code, through dreams and secret symbols. Before you can unite with your other, unknown self, you must work out a language that will be clear and understandable—and you *must* unite with your other self in order to use the powers within you.

You and your subconscious are prisoners in separate cells, tapping out messages to each other through a stone wall of inhibition. Together you could escape your dungeon, but separately you will never break out.

One simple way to break down the wall has been discovered many times by widely different cultures. In various forms, it has been used by witch-doctors in Africa and by the Huna wizards of Polynesia. You may know of it as a game or parlor trick but it can be a telephone line between you and your subconscious.

Make a pendulum by tying a thread about ten inches long to any small object. A ring will do very well. Hold the thread between the thumb and forefinger of one hand

and rest your elbow on a table or the arm of a chair, so the pendulum hangs free. Now, hold the pendulum completely still and say to yourself, "I am about to communicate with my other self. I am consciously holding the pendulum completely still, but my subconscious, which controls all my muscles, will take over and cause the pendulum to swing back and forth." Although you keep your fingers from moving, in a short time the pendulum will begin to swing—just a little at first and then in widening arcs.

Your subconscious mind is controlling tiny muscles in your fingers and hand, with movements too small to register consciously. You have established a true contact. This is *not* a game. At first, as you experiment, you'll find that you can *consciously* cause the pendulum to move by "willing it," even though you don't move your fingers. Naturally, if you *tell* your other self to move the pendulum, it will. You must learn to "let go" consciously, to step back and let your subconscious speak for itself.

But first, you must establish a language. There are four simple movements your pendulum can make: Away and toward you; back and forth in front of you; in a clockwise circle or in a counter-clockwise circle. Two of these movements can be used for indicating "yes" and "no". The third can mean "I don't know" and the fourth can be reserved for times when your other self wants to disagree with you—and there will be such times!

It doesn't matter which movement stands for what answer. You can decide for yourself—but why not let your subconscious choose? Ask your other self to select a movement which will mean "yes," and wait for it to answer. Then, one by one, ask for a movement for the other three possible answers. In this way, you'll be off to a good start in establishing contact.

These four answers *are* limiting, but you'll be surprised at how much information you can get by using them. The trick lies in what you ask, as if you were playing the

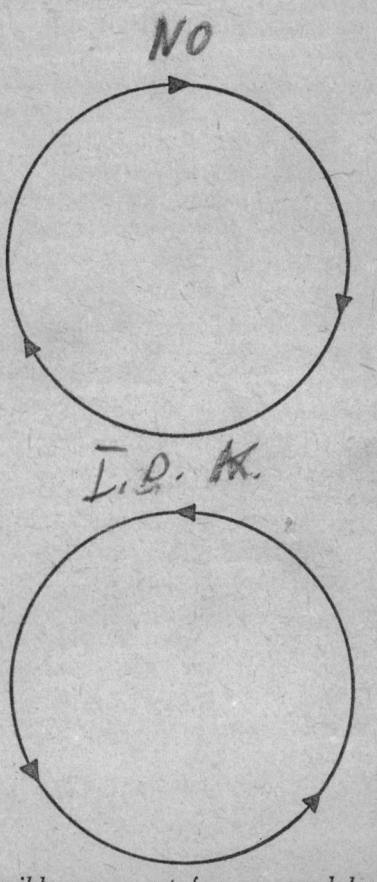

Possible movements for your pendulum

game of Twenty Questions. For instance, here is a sample of the way a question and answer period might go:

Q: Is my overweight caused entirely by physical factors?
A: No.
Q: Is it caused by a recent psychological problem?
A: No.
Q: Is it caused by something that happened in my childhood?
A: Yes.
Q: Am I punishing myself for being "bad" in some way?
A: No.
Q: Am I obeying something someone told me as a child?
A: Yes.
Q: Was it my mother or father?
A: Yes.

This sample is from an actual question-and-answer period. The questioner found that she was still trying to "eat lots of food" so she could "grow up big and strong." Since she was already an adult, there was only one way she could grow—sideways! A single self-hypnotic session erased the faulty conditioning and she began to lose weight. Many psychosomatic problems rest on a ridiculously simple base.

The pendulum is not the most satisfactory way to contact the subconscious, but for the beginner it is the easiest. Later, you may find you have a gift for automatic writing. If you work very well with the pendulum, put a piece of paper on a clipboard and sit in a comfortable chair with the clipboard in your lap. Let the writing hand rest on the paper, lightly holding a pencil. Then tell your subconscious to write what it wants—and "let go" of your hand.

Don't expect anything to happen immediately—just relax and think of something else. Eventually, you may find your hand writing a note to you, "all by itself." Some people find this an excellent method of communicating with their other selves. Only experimentation will show how it works for you.

However, the pendulum is a good tool, simple and reliable—and it's far enough to go, at first, if you're not used to the idea. Coming face-to-face with yourself can be an unsettling experience.

One person who performed this exercise in a joking mood was actually frightened when the pendulum began to move. He was an intelligent man, proud of his knowledge but completely unaware of his other self—or how much more knowledge was available to him, if he only knew where to find it. When he got over his fear, he was delighted with his new friend and spent a good deal of time "talking to himself"—with gratifying results.

Once you've learned this method of freeing your subconscious, you are on your way to a greater understanding of all your mental and physical processes. Remember, your other self controls your muscles and glands as well as your memory.

You may be suffering from an illness that is the result of an inner conflict. Almost certainly, you haven't been able to achieve *all* that you set out to do in life—yet all the people you ever thought you could be are locked inside you, unable to be born.

Next time you don't know what makes you act the way you do, talk it over with yourself.

Points to Remember from Chapter III

1. Before you can unite with your subconscious to set your inner powers free, you must have communication.
2. The pendulum is the simplest and easiest way to communicate with your other self.
3. Depending on the questions you ask, the pendulum

can give you important information on your own motivations.
4. You may be suffering from a physical or psychological ailment that is very easy to cure, if you find the psychological basis for it.
5. Next time you're puzzled by your own motives, ask yourself about it.

Chapter IV

THROW AWAY YOUR CRUTCHES

Few people are strong enough to go through life without certain mental crutches which are used to prop up faltering egos. Chapter I discussed basic limitations which might have been instilled in you as a child. Chief among these is the habit of giving up long before you must.

This habit is called the "don't climb, you'll fall" crutch. As a child you were taught to slow down, to consider the consequences, to look before you leap. Of course, most of these early lessons were for your own good—they kept you from breaking your neck.

But the subconscious, which must have resented being held back, finally learned the lesson too well. And, because the subconscious must have *some* reason for everything it does, it manufactured good excuses to account for this cowardly behavior. This established a strong negative conditioning which fed itself until your other self came to believe it was a good thing never to try as hard as possible, to give up before an issue was in doubt.

You are not alone in this. By the time they've become adults, most men and women use only a small fraction of their energy, their brains or their will to win. It becomes second nature to stop trying, to admit defeat because *if they try, they may fail*. So instead they say, "I'm too old" or "too young" or "too fat" or "too thin." No one can achieve success with his mind geared to failure.

Think of all the times when your "common sense" made you decide to give up a plan because it "couldn't" succeed. In reality your subconscious mind, using the "don't climb, you'll fall" crutch, decided it was better not to try than to run the risk of failure.

It may seem that you can spend a comfortable lifetime plodding along this way, never taking a risk—but the facts are tragically different. It's exactly like having a headache all the time. You can learn to live with it and still function, but you *know* you're not well—and the knowledge is depressing—so you fall into a mental state where nothing matters and slide into negativity.

Of course, by its nature a negative mental state keeps you from generating the desire needed to get out of it. When you're feeling low, it's hard to say, "Well, I've got to feel better now"—and *do* something about it.

In order to overcome your faulty conditioning you must back up your new suggestions with *emotion* and *desire*. Your crutches were built up through the years, but if you impress your other self with enthusiasm you can lose them in days. Remember, a suggestion has no power by itself—it has to be accepted subconsciously. When you no longer submit to your crutches, they'll vanish.

You *can* recondition yourself to use your full potential. Your subconscious *wants* to be free and, as you work toward a better self, the change will be easier because *all* of you is aiding the process.

If you've been using a pendulum, you're beginning to realize how easily things can be accomplished when all of you is involved. Now it's time for another step.

Chapter II discussed a way to improve the memory and relax the body. Here's a method which can also be used for memory development but, like the first system, it's more important as a way to communicate with your other self.

Before you go to sleep at night, close your eyes and imagine a screen—like a motion picture screen—in your mind. When you've established the screen, recall something beautiful you've seen—something with color, like a forest or a sunset—and ask your other self to show it on your screen.

Just as with the memories you called up in Chapter II, you may have to wait a while, but after you get used to this new way of communicating, you'll find your other self can supply visual memories very quickly.

These messages can move in both directions. By showing pictures in your "mind's eye," you have a powerful way to recondition your subconscious into taking a better view of yourself and what you want to accomplish.

Form a picture of yourself—laughing, successful, mature, self-confident. Show that picture on your inner screen and *see it with emotion.* Let your other self know that this is the way you *should* be and the way you *want* to be—project the image with force! Flash that picture on your screen every night before you go to sleep and you'll be surprised at how soon your other self acts on it. Unless you already wake up every morning feeling like a million dollars, you've got a treat in store for you.

There is a poem by William Henley, called "Invictus," in which the last two lines are:

> *"I am the master of my fate:*
> *I am the captain of my soul."*

Be your own captain! See yourself that way. And throw away those crutches—you don't need them!

Points to Remember from Chapter IV

1. Children are taught, "Don't climb, you'll fall," so they can learn caution.
2. By the time they're adults, most people are conditioned never to use their full potential.
3. This is a psychologically dangerous state as it leads to a negative outlook, the forerunner of failure.
4. The way to attack negativity is with emotion, desire and belief.
5. By using the inner movie screen described here, you can see yourself as you *should* be—and force your subconscious to accept the picture.

Chapter V

ALL THE WORLD'S A STAGE

You carry an inner image of what you are in your subconscious and it's this image which influences others, not your external shell. When handsome people are happy and successful, it's because they have a handsome image of themselves which they project to the world. More often, physically attractive men and women are inwardly unhappy because they have a picture of themselves which doesn't match the external view.

There are well-known stories about the movie stars who, with the world at their feet, took to drugs or ended up as suicides; at the same time history records that the fascinating Cleopatra was a small, dark woman with a hook nose, and the Queen of Sheba, who captivated King Solomon of the thousand wives, was better known for her wit than her looks.

There is no question that others are influenced toward you by the way you see yourself. Unfortunately, you probably see yourself through a veil of self-doubt, guilt and fear—the result of childhood conditioning. Remember, every childhood failure took root in your wide-open mind and was filed but not forgotten.

Everyone wants to be more forceful, more dynamic, able to lead and know that others will follow. The answer lies in self-confidence and you can give yourself this trait easily—by learning to daydream with a purpose. All human beings daydream from time to time but without the twist which changes it from a pastime to a power.

First of all, you must realize that any change in personality, any increase in your own magnetism, must come from within *you*. No one can pull anything out of himself that isn't there to start with, but within everyone is a fountain of strength, a secret reservoir of power waiting to be tapped.

You've already discovered through your inner movie screen that your other self is intensely visual—not only can it give you clear-cut memory pictures, but any wish you strongly project on your screen will affect your subconscious.

Now let's digress for a moment. Without realizing it, the majority of people unconsciously think of the reality around them as a kind of play in which they play a part. Six hundred years before William Shakespeare wrote, "All the world's a stage," a Persian poet named Omar Khayyam wrote:

> For in and out, above, about, below,
> 'Tis nothing but a magic picture show,
> Played in a box whose candle is the sun,
> Round which we phantom figures come and go.

Like most poetry, this observation came from the subconscious mind of the poet—it was his own way of expressing his view of reality.

So you play a part—and not only do you play a part, but *you* decide what part you'll play. Consciously or subconsciously, the picture of yourself that you've built up through the years is what you project. If you "cast" yourself as a weakling, others will take you at your own value—and if you see yourself as a star, those around you will treat you like one.

Start using your inner movie screen to see yourself as the leading character in life's drama. Envision those around you as minor or supporting characters who react to *your* speeches and *your* actions.

Every night, act out a little play in your mind. Imagine different situations and see yourself as the star of the show. *See* yourself as you know you should be, doing what you would do if all your dreams came true.

Don't forget why you're doing all this—*you are impressing your subconscious,* conditioning yourself to a permanently positive viewpoint. The situations on your inner screen show you as you *can* be if your other self unlearns the lies it was taught.

Within a few days after you start this exercise, you should be aware of the change in your point of view. Shortly after that, you'll see the change reflected in those around you.

Of course, it doesn't *always* work out that way. One man, who consulted a hypnotherapist for help with his timidity, used this method for a week after he was taught to use his inner movie screen. At the end of that time he stormed into the therapist's office and said, "See here, I've been following your orders for long enough! Now, when am I going to see these great changes in myself?"

At first, he couldn't understand what was so funny. Then the therapist reminded him of the man he had been the week before—a man who would never have had the nerve to question the treatment, whether he was dissatisfied or not. He'd released his own power, and his new self was so natural that he had trouble remembering his old personality.

Never be disappointed if you don't experience an immediate reaction on the conscious level—give your other self time to absorb and understand your desire. Remember that it took years to mold you into your present pattern and you'll be delighted at the change you can see in days.

Someday, someone will ask you for the secret of your self-confidence. But there's no secret. It's just that all the world's a stage. . . .

Points to Remember from Chapter V

1. Other people react to your image of yourself rather than to your exterior behavior.
2. The answer to a more forceful, dynamic personality lies in self-confidence.
3. All the self-confidence and power you need is within you—you just have to call for it.
4. By using your inner movie screen, you can erase your negative conditioning and impress your other self with a picture of you as you *should* be.
5. When you accomplish this, you'll change not only yourself but the way everyone reacts to you.

Chapter VI

...AND A LITTLE CHILD SHALL LEAD THEM

At first, you may find it hard to understand that the subconscious, which is capable of so much, must be influenced like a small child during your reconditioning. But you must remember that only through the proper training of this child can you become a completely whole adult. You'll never free your subconscious powers by just thinking about them on the conscious level.

Max Freedom Long, author of *The Secret Science Behind Miracles,* writes that the Huna magicians of Polynesia believed there are three portions of the human mind: The low self, the middle self and the high self. The middle self corresponded to what we call the conscious mind, the place where a person lives during the waking hours. The high self was a spiritual entity, in contact with all other high selves. It could draw from the accumulated knowledge of all mankind, but had no contact at all with the middle self.

The only way to contact the high self was through the low self, a childish being *which corresponds to what we call the subconscious*. A request for psychic power originating in the middle (conscious) self had to pass through the low (subconscious) self in order to tap the hidden strength of the high self.

This is a very good picture. It *will* help if you think of your subconscious as a small child, gifted with miraculous

SELF-HYPNOSIS 31

powers for good or bad through its ability to harness a strength unavailable to your conscious (middle) mind.

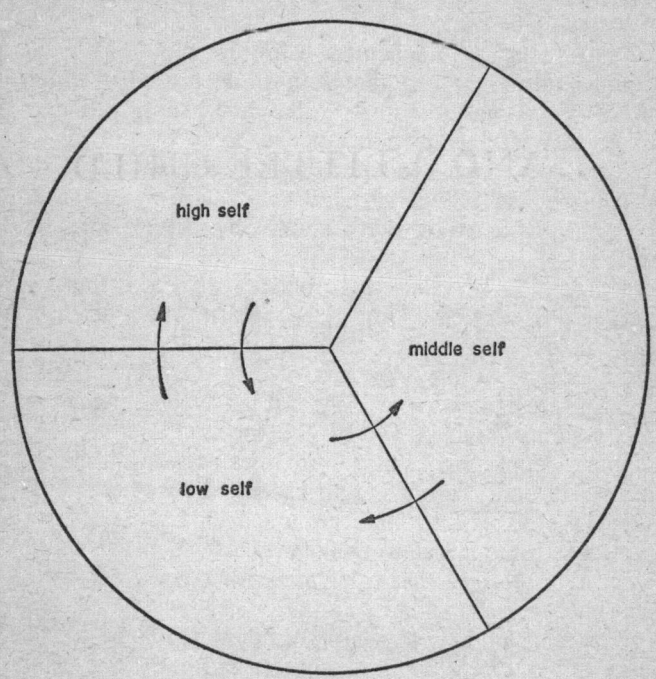

The Huna Divisions Of The Mind

However, your other self is operating on false information so the powers at its command are not being used—or they are being used against you.

The next time you have a headache, get out your pendulum and ask your other self whether it is punishing you. You may be suffering from a simple physical symptom or *you may find you are being punished for breaking some rule you learned as a child*. It's pitiful to think of the number of people in our modern society who stagger through life under the heavy weight of unnecessary guilt, long after they know *consciously* there is nothing to blame themselves for.

One woman who applied for help—Joanne—was overweight, unattractive and disagreeable. Her usual manner toward others was so sarcastic that few people cared to be her friends. Joanne didn't realize there was anything wrong with *her*, but she knew something was wrong. Although she had all the material things she wanted, she was unhappy and she didn't know why. Above all, she was lonely.

Investigation revealed that Joanne was an extremely sensitive girl, very easily hurt. Her sarcasm was a defense, a way of covering up her weakness by telling others she didn't care what they thought of her. Of course, she wasn't aware of this consciously, but her type of person is fairly common—maybe you know someone like her.

Often, people who suffer from these typical negative mechanisms are transparent to everyone but themselves —they are obvious to those around them but their conscious minds are closed to their own motivations. In these cases, it's necessary that the knowledge come from their own subconscious minds.

After learning how to use the pendulum, Joanne found that as an over-sensitive little girl she had been convinced she was bad. When Joanne's mother disapproved of anything, she would call it "wicked," so Joanne learned to think of herself in this way.

Different people would respond to this negative stimulus in different ways. In Joanne's case, she felt she was so bad that people couldn't like her. She responded by over-eating and making herself repulsive—as if to say, "I don't care."

Once Joanne knew the basis of her malfunction, it was necessary to recondition herself in a positive way, which she did by using her inner movie screen. She lost weight

SELF-HYPNOSIS 33

and her new personality made her much more attractive than she had been.

Consciously, Joanne had long ago stopped thinking of herself as a bad little girl, but subconsciously she was still paying for her "wickedness," far into her adult life.

If you get into the habit of using your pendulum whenever you have a headache or feel depressed for "no reason," you'll find many instances when false conditioning has caused you needless pain. Once you find the faulty information, you can use your inner movie screen to recondition yourself. Always use a simple image, be firm but gentle and send your messages with belief.

Trial will quickly show you your own best method, but remember—your other self will appreciate patience and *you have to live* with yourself. Don't expect instant results. Even when the answer to a problem suddenly appears in your conscious mind, your other self has been thinking it over for some time.

Your subconscious can never be a mature individual as we think of the term—it will always be the child in you with miraculous powers. But that child, set free, can lead you to whatever you want in the world.

Points to Remember from Chapter VI

1. You can't free your subconscious powers by just thinking about them on the conscious level.
2. It will help if you think of your other self as a small child with miraculous powers.
3. Often, a headache or other physical symptom is a punishment for some childhood fault your conscious mind forgot long ago.
4. Use your pendulum often to see if any malfunction is caused by negative subconscious conditioning.
5. Once you find the faulty conditioning, you can erase it with positive suggestion.

Chapter VII

THE PATH TO POWER

Several times, previous chapters have referred to forms of magic practiced by different cultures throughout the world. You have seen that no matter what it's called, the power men use to mould the world around them can only come from one place—within themselves. The witch doctor with his magic bones, the medieval witch who tried to summon Satan, and the modern American who sees a hypnotist when he wants to stop smoking are all striving for the same thing—to tap the inexhaustible source of a power they *know* exists somewhere close at hand.

Modern society, with its endless search for security, has come closer to the secret of this power than many previous cultures. At the same time, because of its materialistic viewpoint, today's world has stubbornly refused to recognize the basic facts discovered by people who are considered primitive.

The truth, of course, lies somewhere between a belief in shiny machines and a belief in dancing to the rain god. But, in both of these cases, the key word is *belief*. In all the ways men and women have developed to fill themselves with power, the common factor is a belief that they *can* do it.

Very often, uncomplicated men and women have a grasp of the essential truths which escape more sophisticated people. In a clinic recently, a resident psychologist was surprised to find one of the orderlies, an uneducated man, reading a scientific book on the development of human beings. The orderly looked puzzled and the psychologist asked him about the book, thinking he might have trouble understanding the language.

The orderly looked up with a smile and said, "Has *this* guy got it all wrong!" Seeing the psychologist's surprise, he added, "Here he talks about life being in us. Man, how wrong can you get? Life isn't in *us,* we are in *life.* Life is there, always, whether we take our little piece or not."

The psychologist realized that the other man was right. His uncomplicated view of reality was true—is true of almost anything you experience in this existence. The power you can tap is not just *in* you—it *includes* you and you are part of it. Whether you use it or not, it is there.

Happiness, strength, vitality—these are all part of the natural order of things, existing around you at all times. If you want, think of them as streams running through a country you must cross. The streams are there—you can avoid them completely or you can refresh yourself by plunging in.

The galaxy is full of energy. Across the sky, new stars are being born, midwifed by a blind Creation with power to burn. The same force that can create a star or cause a twig to flower is inside *you!* To release it, you just have to admit it's there and *believe* you can use it.

This is magic—black magic and white! This is what lies behind the Yoga mystic in his Himalayan cave and the Fiji firewalker. This is the path to power and the door you must open to reach that path—the door to the subconscious!

Once you open that door and let your other self go free, you can step across to the stars—or bridge the distance between human souls.

Yet people are so hemmed in by fear that they sometimes think this very fear is a natural and normal force

—a built-in safeguard so they can't use their inner powers until they're wise enough to do it safely. If this was ever true, the safeguard has long outlived its usefulness. In fact, unless modern man can learn to discard it, this proud civilization will go the way of all the others which couldn't become adult—it will destroy itself.

Our poetry and works of art, our pride in achievement, are proof that the power to create *must* find a way to express itself. But how many accomplishments are based on fear and how many in freedom? How many bold things have you done in order to avoid the bravest act of all—the search within you for the source of all accomplishment?

Maybe modern man is afraid the inner power will be too much to handle. Or he may share the mood of that first primitive man who turned away from the burning stars and toward more simple puzzles, like how to keep out of the rain.

Well, humanity learned how to keep out of the rain, but the frontiers are still there, both outward to the stars and inward to the secrets of the mind. There is as great a distance between one human mind and another as between stars, but both ways are open to the searching intelligence.

The following chapters will speak of magic, which was the effort of our ancestors to define a power they could use but not explain. Today, there are too many names for it. You'll have to find your own.

But named or not, you've been set on the secret path to power. Follow it. . . .

Points to Remember from Chapter VII

1. The powers men use to mould the world around them can only come from one place—within themselves.
2. Both primitive and modern methods of utilizing the powers of mind have a common factor—belief.
3. The things you want—like happiness, strength, vitality—are part of the natural order of things. Whether you draw on them or not, they are there.
4. The majority of people would rather attack the most difficult outside problems than explore the mysteries within themselves.
5. The path to power leads through the maze of your own mind. But you *can* follow it.

Chapter VIII

AN INNER MAGIC

At this moment, in a Haitian shack overlooking a sea as heavy as quicksilver, a *papaloi*—a Voodoo man—is squatting within a protective circle of corn meal, which will keep the forces he summons from harming him. He has invoked Baron Samedi, Lord of the Dead, and prayed for strength to Ogun and Saint James, Lords of Fire and Warfare.

Now he takes up a small doll of wax, into which he has pressed hairs and fingernail clippings obtained from his enemy. He whispers the final incantation, having already baptized the doll with his enemy's name. Carefully, he takes a long sliver of iron and drives it through the doll's body.

Now the papaloi can relax. He knows his enemy will die unless he pulls the sliver out of the doll. It may take a day or a week, but the victim will die—with a pain in his belly.

This is not a description of an act which took place a hundred years ago—it is happening *now,* and not only in Haiti. With slightly different ceremonies, it is taking place in every country in the world, as it has since mankind walked upright—and perhaps before.

Magic has always captured the imagination of mankind because of its promise of power. With magic, you can triumph over a hostile world, destroy your enemies and lift yourself above the ranks of your fellow mortals. The concept of "mana"—a South Pacific word meaning supernatural power—is world-wide.

To most people, magic means *black* magic. The belief that one must pay for spiritual power with spiritual coins led to the idea of selling one's soul to the devil—a terrifying thought but a popular one still. In 1964, a Presbyterian minister in Scotland found that Black Masses were being held in the local ruins of a 17th century church. In England in the same year, a graveyard was desecrated for purposes of black magic. The parish rector retaliated by placing a curse on the desecrators.

The fact is, there is only one kind of magic but there are two ways of looking at it. White magic relies on exactly the same principles as black magic. The only difference is its constructive use, to build up rather than tear down. You can use white magic to build a new conception of yourself and make it come true. For no matter what the power is called, you have it in *you.*

SELF-HYPNOSIS 39

The Voodoo man with his doll is sure of his facts. He has done all the proper things and he *believes,* with all his heart and with the assurance that generations before him have done the same things and gotten fast results.

Let's analyze what the papaloi is doing and see how it relates to you. First of all, he has the doll, a *focus.* It's something he understands, a symbol on which he can concentrate. Secondly, he has the ritual, a *formula* which he has followed many times before. Finally, he has *belief,* without which none of the other things would matter.

Belief energizes a wish, gives it body and makes it come true.

The Voodoo man is using the Huna principles mentioned in Chapter VI. He is using the *simplest possible picture* to get the message across to his low self—his subconscious. He doesn't care if the spell is relayed to a high self or to the various spirits he invokes. He works for results.

The child in you—your other self—responds to ritual and belief even when your conscious mind is negative. There are numerous case histories to illustrate this but one dramatic case will suffice.

After years of studying music in the hope of becoming a concert pianist, Helen became the victim of arthritis while still a young woman. Within a short time, her hands were no longer capable of the performance she demanded of them. She herself was no longer a well-adjusted woman but a miserable creature who caused suffering to everyone around her, unable to bear the happiness of others because she could feel none.

Helen was fortunate in having a psychologist friend with an open and unorthodox mind. When he told Helen she was committing psychic suicide, she laughed bitterly and said she had actually considered suicide a year ago, before the start of her affliction. It was an unhappy love affair, she confided, which almost made her take her life with her own hands. Since then, her pain and suffering had made the thought of death very welcome at times.

Her words gave the psychologist a flash of insight—they were an obvious clue to her subconscious state. He asked if she was willing to try magic to help her condition. Helen only hesitated a moment before she said she was willing to try *anything*. No drugs had helped, no exercises had been able to restore agility to her fingers.

The psychologist was a student of the occult. One evening, soon afterward, he met the girl at her apartment. She watched unbelievingly as he unloaded materials from a briefcase. At his request, she clipped off pieces of fingernail which he pressed into the lump of beeswax he was moulding into a pair of hands. He took a couple of drops of blood from her finger and added it to the mixture while she watched. Her interest was now mixed with fear—the ritual was right out of a horror movie.

The psychologist added a pinch of unidentified powder to the concoction, spread a circle of corn meal on the floor and asked her to sit inside. For days, he had been thinking up a suitable spell and now her eyes widened as he squatted outside the circle and said, "Damballah Oueddo, Papa Damballah, Lord of Snakes, make these hands as sinewy as the serpent, as flexible as the serpent, as strong as the serpent in the jungle."

As he spoke, he flexed the wax hands and moved the fingers. The girl was becoming emotionally involved—she was breathing fast, her face mirrored the mixed emotions racing through her mind.

Then the psychologist had her hold the hands and say, "The sin is gone. My hands are good and the sin has passed into these other hands, which are no longer mine." She stopped and he had her repeat it over and over again. Finally, when she broke down and cried hysterically, he took back the wax hands, packed them and everything else back into the briefcase. By the time she recovered, everything was out of sight and he had turned up the lights.

The next morning, she phoned the psychologist and begged him to come to her apartment. When he arrived, she was smiling through her tears as she insisted, "They don't hurt! I can move them."

Gently, the psychologist explained how her illness had come about. The key to the whole problem had occurred to him when she had said she was going to take her life *with her own hands*. Her childlike subconscious, taking every expression literally, had proceeded to punish her—through her hands. The pain she felt was the punishment for a "sinful" thought, and the loss of movement, which probably would have grown until her hands were completely paralyzed, was an effort to keep her hands from damaging her.

There was nothing unusual about Helen's case—hysterical paralysis of one sort or another has been recognized and studied since the first researches of Sigmund Freud. The difference lay in the psychologist's unorthodox treatment—and her quick recovery.

If Helen had known about the pendulum, or any other way of communing with herself, she might have gone to the heart of the problem at the beginning of her "illness." She might have been spared all the suffering that followed.

But she was a skeptic and would have laughed at the idea of her other self at that time. This was why the psychologist had gone through the ritual of the spell. Even though she was desperate, willing to try anything, he knew she had to believe something *outside* herself was causing a cure at the same time she was impressing her subconscious by saying, "The sin is gone, my hands are good."

The key was *belief!* The ancient Hebrews originated the idea of the scapegoat—they ritually transferred the sins of the tribe into a goat and then drove the animal over a cliff so that the sins would perish. In certain African tribes right now, there is a witch-doctor called the sin-eater, who takes upon himself the sins of the others and gets rid of them by magic. Religions which practice the ritual of confession are freeing the subconscious of the sense of sin by the same methods.

Many of your own problems are caused by a subconscious which is uncontrolled and destructive, but you can cure yourself. You can free yourself through the power within you—an inner magic.

Points to Remember from Chapter VIII

1. The principles of magic and the belief in it are common throughout the world.
2. White and black magic utilize the same power—the difference lies in whether they are used for positive or negative purposes.
3. The power of magic lies in the subconscious mind and is activated by belief.
4. Many cultures rid themselves of "evil" by a magic casting-out of "sin," which is negativity.
5. You have a personal magic of your own, an inner magic which is only waiting for you to free it.

Chapter IX

YOU *CAN* CONQUER PAIN

In the second century after Christ, hundreds of martyrs died smiling, as spikes were driven through their hands and feet. Witnesses said they seemed to feel no pain as they blessed their murderers.

A few centuries later, thousands of people were convicted of witchcraft—practiced against the teachings of these same martyrs—and burned alive. Some of them *believed* they had signed a pact with Satan. These people laughed as they were burned alive, yelling curses at the good folk who watched.

Right now, on an island in the Indian Ocean, a native boy is being initiated into manhood. During the ceremony, he walks casually across a bed of glowing coals. His feet are not even blistered when he reaches the other side.

In a large American city, a man walks away from his wrecked car, thankful to be alive. He won't notice his broken finger for almost an hour. A few blocks away, another man is cursing the pain of an inflamed hangnail.

While scientists are still uncertain of how pain is caused in the body, they know where it occurs—in the brain! If you hit your finger with a hammer, it isn't your finger that actually hurts. You feel no pain until a nerve-ending sends a message to your brain saying there's been an injury. Then, your *mind* creates a pain-feeling to tell you that you've been hurt.

There is no question that the subconscious mind can refuse to accept pain signals sent to the brain. When this happens, *there is no pain.* Those under the influence of a powerful emotion—the dedicated fervor of the martyr, the schizophrenic frenzy of the "witch," the conviction of the fire-walker—are temporarily above the weaknesses of the flesh. Their *belief* can make them godlike—and you'll notice that the God involved is not any particular one.

The *National Geographic Magazine* for April, 1966, documents the yearly ordeal of a Ceylonese named Mahotty, who pierces his body with needles and pulls a heavy cart roped to hooks in his back. When Mahotty was a young man, his father was falsely accused of murder. Mahotty swore to endure the hooks and needles every year if his father were freed, and he has done so for sixteen years.

The author of the *Geographic* article witnessed Mahotty's ordeal, saw him pull a cart around a village courtyard by huge steel hooks imbedded in the flesh of his back. Later, the Ceylonese walked four times across a burning bed of coals, twice with his young son on his shoulders. His feet were not blistered and his skin showed no signs of prior hook-marks. Every year he heals completely, without a mark.

When asked for his "secret," Mahotty replied, "Faith, total faith in my gods." He is a Hindu.

Even from a purely physical standpoint, pain is neither a reliable nor a constant sense. The nerves capable of registering pain are scattered unevenly throughout the body. If you stick a pin in a spot which has no "pain" nerves, you'll feel nothing, although it may look as though you're causing yourself great pain. Some fakirs of India—the phonies, not the real holy men—use this method. By experimentation, they find painless areas in different parts of their bodies and amaze tourists by sticking pins through these spots.

Recently, medical men have been studying the "pain threshold" in different people—the point at which a "feeling" stops being a nuisance and begins to hurt. Some people have a much higher pain threshold than others, as any doctor knows. In a recent article, an ophthalmologist called attention to the fact that some of his patients have no trouble adjusting to contact lenses while other "nervous" types can't learn to ignore them and constantly feel irritation.

We know that keeping the mind on something else can often "short-circuit" a pain message before it reaches the conscious mind. The pain is still there, but all the lines of communication are tied up and the message can't get through. Millions of men scrape a few millimeters of flesh off their faces every morning—usually while they hum a tune and think of what they're going to do that day. Shaving is actually a painful process and the facial skin remains tender no matter how many times this operation is performed. Yet, because of conditioning and familiarity, Mr. American Male thinks nothing of shaving once or twice a day. He has learned to "turn off" the pain—to raise his pain threshold, just as a local anaesthetic does.

In 1965, workers at Massachusetts General Hospital in Boston reported good results in combating pain in terminal cancer patients. They did this by planting electrodes in selected parts of a patient's brain and running a weak electric current through them. Any pain impulses sent to the brain were short-circuited.

This would appear to be a triumph for physical science, but other researchers working with terminal cancer patients have achieved the same results by using the psychodelic drug *lysergic acid diethylamide*—LSD. After taking LSD and experiencing the consciousness—expanding properties of the drug, the patients not only could suppress their terrible pain but were able to face death without fear.

Your mind can kill pain without external means. LSD is just a short-cut to a point of view which can be reached without drugs. Remember, your other self has control of all your nerves and muscles—it can cut off any given nerve impulse.

It's easier to learn this method while pain isn't actually present, so try it the next time you have a few minutes to spare. First of all, relax your body and your mind so that you'll have a channel to your subconscious. If you've been working with your pendulum or using any of the methods described in earlier chapters, this should be very easy for you.

Now, pick a good strong image to impress your other self. Imagine that in your brain there is a large fuse box, with wires running to all parts of your body. These wires carry the pain messages. Work on this until you can actually *see* the fuses, and the wires running to different portions of yourself.

Picture a wire running from one of your hands to a particular fuse—and see yourself unscrewing the fuse! As the fuse unscrews, you will feel your hand becoming numb. When you have unscrewed it entirely, pinch the "disconnected" hand with your other hand. You'll find it's like pinching a piece of leather—you'll feel pressure but no pain.

When the experiment is over, don't forget to screw the fuse back in. As a rule, pain serves a useful purpose in the body and you don't want to leave part of you "disconnected" without a good reason. In cases where there is unavoidable pain for some time, though, you may find it practical to keep part of you—like a tooth—turned off for quite a while.

As in everything else, the speed with which you master this technique depends on how strongly you impress your other self. Search for other strong images which have impact. The method described gives excellent results, but you may find others which work better for you as an individual. Use your pendulum to test your other self, finding the images which have the greatest impact on you. Remember, what you are learning is a way to alter your whole being, not just a small part of you.

The more often you use your other self, the easier it will be to influence your world, both outside and inside your body. As your subconscious learns what you want, it will work to please you. You *can* conquer pain—but once you do, you'll realize this is not a goal in itself but only another guidepost on your path to power.

Points to Remember from Chapter IX

1. Medical history is full of examples which prove that under strong emotional stimulus, pain need not be felt at all.
2. Pain does not exist until the brain accepts a pain impulse which is sent along a nerve.
3. Doctors have managed to "short-circuit" pain impulses physically, but this has also been achieved with LSD, a drug which is not a pain-killer but a consciousness-expanding agent.
4. By using simple methods to impress your other self, you can cut yourself off from pain.
5. The mastery of pain is not an end in itself but simply another milestone along your path to power.

Chapter X

THE PAIN WITHIN

Although physical pain can be one of the most overpowering forces in life, there are other kinds of pain that are no less destructive to the personality.

Pain is a conditioner; governments that make use of brainwashing know this. The art of reconditioning a prisoner no longer relies on broken bones and twisted limbs. Instead, master psychologists delve into the prisoner's mind, looking for weak spots in his makeup. With these weaknesses for tools, they can remold a man completely, for no bodily torture can match the pain of a wounded mind.

Rather than face an unpleasant memory or an uncomfortable truth, most people will promptly "gloss over" the experience—either partially or totally.

Embarrassment, for instance, is painful. If you try to think of an experience in which you were terribly embarrassed, you'll find either that you can't quite remember the details—your other self is sparing you the pain of remembrance—or that your mind veers away from the incident, refusing to dwell on it.

Actually, large parts of all your experiences are denied to you because of this "protection." One of the ways we humans advance is by learning from our mistakes, and you can't learn if you don't allow yourself to think about them.

Try an experiment. Think of the most embarrassing thing that ever happened to you. Your other self may refuse to give you the experience, but you can use one of the techniques described earlier in this book to bring it into your conscious mind. When you have the memory, go through the whole thing consciously. Don't miss a detail.

Painful, isn't it? Now do it again, immediately—go through the whole experience again, right from the start. This time you'll notice that it doesn't hurt so much—it's lost some of the original impact. Now go through it for the third time.

By the time you've run through the experience three or four times, the pain will have vanished. You'll be in possession of a memory which you were denying yourself—and from which you can learn.

Re-living an experience several times "wears down" the emotion connected with it—there is less pain and more reflection. *There is no sorrow or mental pain that cannot be overcome in this way.* And once you've turned this method into one of your conscious tools, there is a storehouse of useful material at your command.

The same technique can be used *before* an emotional experience. Let's say you're facing an interview which you dread. Try "seeing" it in advance, in any form it could take. Re-play it several times and you'll find that a good deal of the emotional anxiety is gone. Nothing packs the same punch after you've been through it four or five times as it did the first time around.

When using this method for the future instead of the past, it's best to imagine just a few minutes of the experience at a time. If you are at all nervous about a coming event, your other self will try to lure you away from the picture and you'll be side-tracked into a daydream or another thought entirely. Whenever you have trouble keeping your mind on a subject that you consciously like, it's because your other self—for reasons of its own—finds it distasteful.

Don't lose track of the fact that your other self will try to get out of an unpleasant task, just as a child would. That's why *you*—your conscious mind—must be in control of your subconscious powers and not the reverse. Letting your other self guide your destiny alone is like putting a child at the wheel of an ocean liner—no matter how conscientious, he needs someone to tell him where to steer.

Your subconscious learned early that the way to get out of an unpleasant experience was to make it painful—in advance. How many times have you steered clear of an obligation because the very thought of it was painful? Or put off a phone call because you just *knew* it would be unpleasant? The next time you face a task that must be done—one that you've been avoiding—think about it until you know exactly what you find distasteful.

Then *imagine that situation,* no matter how it makes you cringe. Do it a couple of times. You'll soon be able to face the actual situation without fear—because it is no longer capable of giving you mental pain.

This method has been used to undo the faulty conditioning of a lifetime. In one such case, a man named Larry was painfully shy. In his thirties, Larry was unmarried and almost friendless because he'd get tongue-tied in the presence of strangers—he'd "choke up," and couldn't carry on a conversation. Larry was aware of the situation—even the job he chose for his life's work was one in which he met as few people as possible.

Larry *knew* that whenever he had to meet people, he was going to make a fool of himself. In public, the feeling was so strong that usually he couldn't say a word. Even when he talked about the problem, his face became flushed and he twisted in his chair. Obviously, the subject was painful to him.

Larry was told to go home and imagine the most embarrassing situation he could think of, to experience it over and over again. He was dubious about this course as he frequently *did* imagine such things, and it was hardly a pleasant experience. However, he agreed to try *repetition*.

About a week later, Larry wasn't quite a new man, but there *was* a change in him. With a shamefaced grin, he admitted that for years he's suffered from the familiar nightmare of suddenly appearing naked in front of a huge crowd of people. The image was so painful that the mere thought of it made him perspire.

Larry spent several nights dwelling on this situation, although at first he didn't think he could stand it. However, he persevered and, after a few times, the picture didn't seem as horrible as it did at first. Finally, as he began to imagine all the things that could happen, it became funny. This was the turning point—if you can laugh at your fears, they'll fall apart.

At about the same time, Larry found that he was no longer afraid of making a fool of himself in public. While he wasn't ready to be the life of the party, he was beginning to feel he could lead a fairly normal life.

Later, after Larry's shyness had almost vanished, he was able to trace—through a pendulum—the negative conditioning at the base of his phobia. In punishing him as a boy, Larry's father had once called him a fool and said he'd never be able to make his way in a world where he had to deal with people. It was as simple as that—and it wasted years of Larry's life *because he couldn't talk it over with himself*.

Larry is a husband and father now. He stayed in the same business, but his new self-confidence has boosted him out of his old job and into a much better-paying one. He enjoys meeting people and they enjoy meeting him.

Probably he'll continue climbing—success brings success. Although he couldn't realize it, most of his psychic energy was taken up, day after day, with the ceaseless fight against himself. At the present, he is just becoming aware of abilities he hasn't even begun to use.

The most remarkable feature of Larry's case is its lack of originality. Anyone who deals with humanity's psychological ailments could tell you stories of people similarly troubled. Without treatment, the condition can be crippling—but the treatment is not only available, it is knocking on the door of your mind at any given moment.

Once you crack the wall between you and your other self, you are not solving any single problem—you are on your way to solving all of them.

Points to Remember from Chapter X

1. Although physical pain is a powerful negative conditoiner, mental pain can be more destructive to the personality.
2. People's minds tend to "gloss over" an unpleasant memory by forgetting it, which deprives them of useful experience.
3. The sting can be taken out of unpleasant memories by reliving them over and over again, until the emotion is rubbed off.
4. The same technique can be applied to future experiences which are unpleasant but necessary.
5. This technique is most important because it breaks down more of the wall between you and your other self. When you break that wall, you are not solving any single problem—you are on your way to solving all of them.

Chapter XI

WORD MAGIC

Since men first developed language, they have been fascinated by the mystic power and meaning of words. We have come a long way from the creatures who originally put sounds into meaningful patterns—and we have forgotten a great deal—but words still retain their power for us and whoever can wield them still holds a sort of magic.

Words are symbols, and putting an idea into words—either written or spoken—goes a long way toward making it real. To the ancients, much closer to the beginning of speech than we are, this was obvious. In Hebrew, the verb "to name" means the same as "to make appear"—and some inspired writer wrote long ago, "In the beginning was the word."

Even more than other words, proper nouns—the names of individuals—have always been given special significance. In many primitive tribes, individuals do not reveal their true names to anyone but close relatives. Everyone else knows them only by a nickname, for a true name carries power over the owner—the name has a magic connection with the person.

In modern India, an infant is given two names during the naming ceremony. One of these is for public use and the other will never be known by anyone but loved ones.

The history of magic—black or white—is full of the

importance of words. One summons a demon by name, speaking secret words of power to bind him and make him serve. All formulas for witchcraft clearly indicate that certain words must be repeated again and again— power-sounds to draw a force from the void and put it at the service of the speaker. This has its parallel in the prayer of the Tibetan monk, who chants, "Om mane padme om," again and again. The words are supposed to echo through the world as soon as spoken.

To the monks, it doesn't matter if the words are spoken aloud or written, so they use devices called prayer-wheels. These are small wheels set in streams, like the water wheels used for power to turn mill stones in other cultures. A prayer-wheel has a piece of paper attached to each spoke, on which is written a prayer. As the stream turns the spokes, the prayer is sent out into the world.

Words are halfway between the wish and the fulfillment. The folklore of all nations is filled with stories of the poor peasant who comes to power through saying the right thing, literally or symbolically. The story of Ali Baba, who stood before the cave and shouted "Open, sesame!" is a thinly disguised allegory showing how the use of words can lead to wealth.

In both primitive and sophisticated societies, there is an underlying, often hidden belief that some words are packed with power. To this day, people in countries all over the world are fearful of mentioning death or disease —they believe that to mention the thing will cause it to happen.

As for you, you may often have said, "Speak of the devil and he appears"—laughingly, of course, because you mentioned a friend who suddenly arrived. But the phrase you use is an old warning, born in fear. According to the old belief, Satan himself will come if you call him three times. And in old Norse tales, witches caused storms by standing on a high hill and calling the winds by name.

SELF-HYPNOSIS 55

All of this background has a direct bearing on the purpose of this chapter. It applies to your subconscious, with its primitive, literal interpretation of everything, for in your other self is huddled every superstition that the race of man ever evolved to ward off a pitiless destiny. You have already seen how this child within you acts on what your conscious mind *says,* not necessarily what it *means.* But you are probably not aware of how this has affected you in the past or may be affecting you now.

One person unaware of the "magic" he was practicing on himself was Harry, who suffered from a chronic upset stomach for which several doctors could find no physical cause. Harry was a successful contractor, happy with his profession and his progress in it. Seemingly, there was no psychological reason for the illness which was causing him to lose weight and ruining his digestion.

In talking of his home life, Harry said he had been married for many years, had a child whom he loved and was apparently well-adjusted in his marriage. But, as he revealed his story, a pattern became clear.

Harry started in life as a laborer and worked his way up by sheer hard work and determination. Now, in his middle years, he was enjoying the fruit of his labors—he had a big house, a fat bank account and luxury he'd never imagined in his youth.

His wife, Ruth, had worked with him all the way and was likewise pleased with their progress. But, unlike Harry, she had social ambitions. She wanted to entertain, to show off the success they had made for themselves, while Harry preferred to take his shoes off and relax with a few beers at the end of a working day.

When asked about Ruth's ambitions, Harry's reaction was quick and definite. "I can't stand that stuff," he said. "We never needed it before and we don't now. Besides, those society people are all phonies—they make me sick to my stomach."

Harry had probably said these words a hundred times

without realizing that he was telling himself the cause of his sickness at the same time he caused it. He *still* didn't understand, but once the words were spoken, the whole thing became clear. He had repeated "—they make me sick to my stomach" so often that he had set up a conditioning process—his other self had obliged!

Through the pendulum, Harry found that his distaste for a social life was based on fear. A proud and self-reliant man, he was afraid that he and Ruth would not measure up to a more "high-class" environment. So he over-reacted, insisting that he didn't like the people and using an unfortunate choice of words to express his feeling.

Harry's background in contracting had given him a strongly visual mind—he had no trouble using the movie screen technique described in Chapter IV. Within a few days, he was amusing himself with pictures of Ruth entertaining lavishly. As a matter of fact, when they actually started giving parties, he found that he enjoyed himself immensely. At the same time, his stomach trouble cleared up completely. He had withdrawn the order at the base of his illness.

Harry's case is one out of thousands. Another man in similar circumstances used to say his work constantly irritated him. He had a rather painful skin infection too, and no idea of how it was caused.

You may be subjecting yourself to aches and pains or even serious disorders for reasons that are just as obvious, once they are explained. How often have you said that something gave you a pain in the neck? Is there anything that makes you tired?

You needn't begin watching your language carefully for every expression that could do you harm—this chapter shouldn't be a headache to you! But, when you find yourself using such expressions, be *sure* your other self doesn't take you literally.

It's a good idea to talk to your other self at least once

SELF-HYPNOSIS 57

a day, and a good question to ask is "Have I said anything today which could cause me physical or mental harm?" You'll be surprised at what you find.

Within a short time, your other self will learn the difference between an expression you don't mean literally and one you do. But don't forget to keep checking—the pain you avoid will make it worthwhile.

This chapter has covered the negative aspect of words—the harm they can do in the childlike mind of the other self. The next chapter will discuss some magic words for good, and what they can do for you.

As in black and white magic, the only difference is how the words are used, but the method is the same—words are thoughts on their way to becoming matter.

Points to Remember from Chapter XI

1. From the beginning of language, men have always given magic power to words.
2. In the most modern societies, there is an underlying, often hidden belief that some words are packed with mystic power.
3. Your other self, on its primitive level, causes many of your unintended but spoken orders to come about.
4. This can induce physical and mental discomfort or even serious disorders.
5. By using a pendulum regularly, you can "erase" these unintentional orders before your subconscious acts on them.

Chapter XII

SUPERCHARGE YOUR OTHER SELF WITH LOVE

In Chapter XI, you saw how words of power can summon up sickness or even death. But you can see that words of power are only powerful because they appeal to your other self. *Any* strong communication between yourself and your subconscious will do the trick, whether it is by word, picture or simply a powerful emotion.

In his autobiography, Benvenuto Cellini tells how, as a young boy, he saw something in the flames of the family fireplace one night. He called his father, who looked at what seemed to be a tiny, lizardlike animal, dancing in the midst of the flames.

As little Benvenuto stared in awe at the flickering creature, his father hit him sharply on the side of the head. Then, as the boy cried, he gathered him into his arms.

"My son," he said, "I have done this so you will never forget—you have seen a salamander, a mystic creature which lives in fire and brings luck to the household it visits."

Cellini's father knew something that scientists were to hail as a great discovery hundreds of years later—the subconscious will judge *anything* by the strength of the emotion attached to it. Because Cellini was struck without warning as he watched the salamander, the experience was indelibly printed on his mind.

Cellini never did forget the incident—not just because

SELF-HYPNOSIS

of the salamander, but because his father had taught him a great truth. He revealed this truth to the world when he wrote his autobiography in 1558, but apparently no one thought much of the knowledge until the twentieth century, when behavioral psychologists re-discovered it in an accepted, "scientific" manner.

Good images are just as strong as bad ones. Because of negative conditioning, most people feel more emotional impact from words like hate, jealousy and greed than words like love, kindness and compassion. Yet these, too, are words of power, more capable of re-making the world than any war.

All the great prophets and saints whose words we remember emphasized that emotion is a *force*, not just a feeling. They knew that emotion, concentrated and *believed in, impresses the part of us which can, in turn, impress others.*

When you're really angry, your emotion makes you powerful because you project it. Your other self picks up a simple, easily understood picture of yourself in a rage —aptly called a towering rage, as it seems to give you stature—and amplifies it.

Your anger impresses the people around you, since everyone reacts to a strong emotion, and your subconscious makes a note that something pleasant happens when you're angry. After that, you may find yourself becoming angry more often, for the sense of power it gives you.

But anger or hate, being negative, always consume the person who is addicted to them, and they eventually destroy the capacity for positive emotions or goals. We know many people who are anger-addicts, who need rage because it makes them feel strong, and every one of them suffers from one or more psychosomatic disorders.

Your other self does *not* want to hate—it does *not* want to be negative. If you persist in feeding it on negative forces, it will protest in a way that's likely to be personally uncomfortable to you.

You can feel love or kindness as strongly as any other emotion, and your subconscious will pay you back in the same coin you give it. Think of a situation that invariably makes you angry or irritated. Go over it again and again in your mind, as described in Chapter X, until you've worn out the emotion. Then, inject love and understanding into the vacancy.

Make it strong. If it's a person who annoys you, dwell on some good characteristic which makes that person a worthwhile individual. Everyone has some good qualities —including yourself. You'll find that your other self responds to a strong suggestion of love just as well as any other stimulus.

Some people are afraid that a feeling of love, or even good nature, will be taken as a sign of weakness, an invitation to hurt them. If you're one of these people, remember this: *You cannot live without entering life.* If you want, you can pass through your whole existence shielding your delicate psyche from any sudden jars—but you'll never experience the joy of fully committing yourself to anything and you'll never be fully alive.

Don't be afraid of the bad in others. In every human being, love is struggling to be born, held back only by the same fear that slows its growth in yourself. People who are not actively good are not necessarily bad, only slow to recognize the positive forces in themselves.

In India, where love and hate are very well understood, a holy man greets every living creature with the words, "I salute the divinity in you," whether it be a man or a cobra. It is an affirmation of the fact that each of us harbors an inner flow of divinity, of positive power. In some, it is a mighty river—in others, a stream blocked by the debris of faulty conditioning and negative emotions.

But the core is there and it can't help but respond to the same feeling in others. Commit yourself to love and understanding—and if your commitment sometimes brings you sadness, remember what Kahlil Gibran said about happiness—you can only hold it in the hollow carved out by pain. Until it passes through the fire of pain, the soul presents a shallow surface, unable to hold anything.

Begin with love. When you've filled yourself with this positive emotion, you'll find that health, wealth and success are also words and symbols of power. If you've been concentrating on these goals in a negative way, you'll achieve little even if they come to you—the world is full of rich and unhappy people. Though money can solve many problems, only a fool believes it's the answer to *everything*.

If you fill yourself with strong, positive feeling, everything you achieve will reflect your own inner joy. But what shall it profit you to gain the whole world if you lose the inner well-spring of your happiness?

Feel love as strongly as you've felt anger—and every thing you learn from this book will be twice as effective. Supercharge yourself with love—your other self will run much better on this mixture than on the thin fuel of frustration and anger.

Points to Remember from Chapter XII

1. Words and symbols of power can summon positive results as well as negative ones.
2. As long as you make a powerful impression, your subconscious will act on *anything* you feed it, good or bad.
3. Most people run the risk of becoming addicted to anger because it's obviously "strong," but this negative emotion can destroy them.
4. Many people are afraid to love because it seems

"weak," but by shutting out love they lose most of what's worthwhile in life.
5. Unless you can commit yourself to giving joy, you'll never be able to fully enjoy anything you accomplish.

Chapter XIII

ANY SUGGESTIONS?

From the time you are born until your sorrowing relatives decide which mortuary will have you, suggestion rules your destiny.

When you were young, your mind was defenseless, completely open—everything you heard or saw affected you in a way far out of proportion to its importance. For this reason, things you learned as a child can stay with you all your life while something you learned last week is often forgotten.

Later, when you became an adult, your mind became less resilient, less open to stimuli. This is supposedly a "normal" part of maturity. Unfortunately, it carries with it a tendency to develop a closed mind against anything new. There are, however, many examples of famous men and women who have kept a youthful viewpoint while benefitting from their accumulated years of experience, and with this book you can join their ranks.

Whether your mind is open or closed, your other self is accepting impressions twenty-four hours a day, even when you're asleep—in fact, even when you're unconscious!

SELF-HYPNOSIS

Recently, experiments were conducted at a midwestern hospital, using two patients who were undergoing identical operations. In both cases, the patients were completely anaesthetized. In one case, the operation was conducted in a "normal" manner, with the doctors chatting to each other about golf, their busy schedules and the general health of the patient.

In the other case, no one spoke but the doctor performing the operation—and he spoke to the patient. His speech went something like this: "All right, Pete, I'm opening you up now—of course, you don't feel a thing. Ah, here's the organ that's been causing all the trouble. I'm taking it out now and you'll probably start to feel better right away. Yes, it's a good thing you got rid of this —you'll be a new man in no time."

Both these patients were about the same age and in the same state of health. Both operations were equally successful. But—after the operations were completed, all similarity ended.

The man whose operation was conducted in the "normal" manner recovered "normally." That is, there were the usual minor setbacks and complications but his improvement was slow and steady.

The other man, to whom the doctor talked personally and reassuringly, enjoyed a phenomenal recovery. He was up and around almost immediately and left the hospital days before the poor fellow with the "normal" operation.

Remember, both men were completely unconscious during their operations. But the subconscious—which never sleeps—recorded everything that happened. In one case, the childlike other self responded to the doctor's reassurance and promoted a swift healing. In the other case the subconscious responded to indifference with indifference, to the disadvantage of the patient.

Some psychologists believe that human beings are simply a mass of conditioned reflexes, motivated by a few simple desires and easily controlled by a direct appeal to these. While there is evidence that people are not quite so simple, this kind of direct suggestion can be seen any day or night on your television screen.

Television advertising, like most other kinds, tries to convince you that you *need* a certain product. If you'll recall, a few years ago, the emphasis was on the *negative* side. Commercials insisted you would be a failure—socially or in business—if you didn't use a particular product.

These were crude attempts, making use of fear to bully the audience. However, even the advertising industry has begun to realize how much more can be done with *positive* conditioning. In the last few years, the emphasis has completely changed. You're no longer told how bad you'll look or smell if you *don't* use a product. Instead, you're told how wonderful life will be if you *do* use it.

Girls are told that if they change their hair color, popularity and marriage are right around the corner. Housewives are told they can keep their husbands interested by using something to soften their hands. Businessmen are assured they'll be more successful and wealthy if they use a certain hair lotion or mouthwash.

Obviously, the advertisers who spend millions of dollars a year on psychological research have found that the subconscious responds more to a promise of love and success than to a threat of failure. Why not take advantage of their expensive experiments and use the same technique on yourself?

Although science is just beginning to work seriously with the powers of the other self, experiments have already been performed which are both fascinating and conclusive. One such experiment was conducted by the Religious Research Foundation in California.

Identical seeds were planted in two separate plots of land, with everything being equal—the same amount of sunshine, type of soil, etc. As the seedlings began to grow, members of the Foundation *prayed* over the two plots. At one they prayed for non-growth, for sickness and disease. At the other they prayed for healthy, sturdy plants.

Shifts were assigned so that there were always several people on duty, aiming their prayers at the plants. The theory was that a number of people working together could direct a stream of thought strong enough to be effective—and it worked!

The plants receiving the benefit of "positive" prayer shot up immediately; they were healthy and strong. Those with "negative" prayer directed at them wilted, then withered. Since everything else was equal, it seems obvious that the difference lay in *concentrated suggestion*.

In these and other experiments, scientists are proving that suggestion guides the destinies of everything alive and able to respond to stimuli. Certainly, you yourself fulfill both these requirements.

Creating a new emotional condition within yourself is, in a sense, selling your subconscious on a more satisfying way of life—and, with this selling job, you can quickly see the results. Just as in advertising, you are convincing your other self that the old product—negativity—has never done the job that the new product—a positive outlook—can do. This is why you must always speak to your subconscious in simple, forceful terms.

Here's a demonstration of how easily you can condition your other self. Stand up, with your arms relaxed at your sides. Take in a slow, deep breath through your nose, with your mouth tightly closed. Take the air down into your abdomen, feel it filling out the space under your ribs. Don't let your shoulders rise—if they do, you're taking the air into your chest, not your abdomen.

Now, let the breath out through your mouth, explosively—make it puff! Count to ten while taking the breath in and release it all at once.

Tell yourself you are taking in energy and optimism with each breath, while you expel negativity every time you exhale. Say it out aloud to your other self. After breathing this way three or four times, you'll find that your spirits *are* lifted, that you feel lighter, physically and mentally.

This is the result of hyperoxygenation, a surplus of oxygen in the blood, renewing the flow of energy to your brain and your body. If not done to excess, this is an excellent exercise. But unless you have built up slowly, too much deep breathing can produce unconsciousness. Be sure to stop when you begin to feel a tingling throughout your body.

Although there's a physical reason for your "lift," your other self will associate the feeling with your suggestion that you're releasing negativity while you take in energy. You are selling a product—optimism—to your own subconscious. When your other self can *feel* a lift at the same time you suggest optimism, you've established a reflex—and sold the product.

Soon, you'll be able to "trigger" yourself, to alter your state of mind and body by simply taking a few deep breaths and investing in a moment's thought, for the energy you accumulate can be used in many different ways.

Now you have another way to condition your subconscious at will.

Any suggestions?

Points to Remember from Chapter XIII

1. Suggestion rules the lives of everyone, whether people realize it or not.
2. Even when you're asleep—or unconscious—your subconscious is absorbing data and reacting to it.
3. The advertising industry, among others, has discovered what can be accomplished by a direct appeal to the desires of the subconscious.

SELF-HYPNOSIS 67

4. Experiments have proved that even plants respond to concentrated suggestion, for good or bad.
5. By using the same type of suggestion, you can "sell" yourself on optimism, self-confidence and success.

Chapter XIV

BELIEVE AND ACHIEVE

Through the history of mankind there have been a handful of individuals whose personal magnetism was so strong they were able to sway nations and control the lives of thousands of people. Without exception, these men and women shared a particular trait—a belief in themselves and their own strength.

These exceptional people have not always been good, for the power they possessed is not limited to the pure in heart. It has been seen in such widely different personalities as Jesus Christ and Napoleon Bonaparte, Gautama Buddha and Adolf Hitler. The force of minds like these can alter the course of history—and, though some of them are responsible for much of what is good in mankind, we're lucky that they don't appear more often than they do.

Much more common are the people all around us—maybe you know one—who have a personal magnetism that few can resist. They may be confidence men or captains of industry, housewives or politicians. Again, what they have in common is an unshakeable belief in themselves.

The force these people wield is called charisma, the ability to exercise authority. In its most powerful form, it can be felt and transmitted like a physical power, for those who possess it can pass it on to their followers.

Jesus could lay hands on his disciples and tell them to go forth and preach—and those ignorant farmers and fishermen *were* able to preach and work miracles. The power passed on to them was a tangible thing, so unmistakable that Paul was able to ask, "Received ye the spirit?" as definitely as if it were a loaf of bread.

Mohammed had the power—he gave his followers a sense of mission so strong that they conquered a large portion of the world to spread his word.

Hitler swayed a nation with a distorted message strong enough to overcome all decency. He spread a sickness throughout his country with his power and most of Germany followed him joyfully, intoxicated by his evil dream.

Most politicians and statesmen have this personal magnetism to a degree. The late President John F. Kennedy had it, as anyone who ever heard or watched him could see, and his death was shattering to those who had experienced directly the impact of his personality.

The quality of charisma is well known to historians and psychologists. Books have been written about personal magnetism and those who possess it. But invariably, the writers ignore one important point. *Everyone has this power and is capable of using it.*

Of course, few can boost their personal power to the point of ruling nations—or would want to. But for most people, success in their personal and business lives is sufficient. By following a few simple exercises, you can strengthen your charisma to a point where the difference is obvious to yourself and everyone around you. The following case history will demonstrate what can be done.

Dick worked for a large corporation, had been with them for some time and was doing work which called for intelligence and common sense. Yet, at the time he finally realized he had a problem, Dick had been in the same position for several years while men hired after him were promoted to executive jobs. The fact was that Dick couldn't *push*—he was well-liked and valued by the firm, but other men took the spotlight away from him at any company meeting—and got the credit that might have been his.

Dick wanted to be hypnotized—he thought that hypnosis could turn him into a tiger, a forceful, dominant man who could take charge of any situation. But it wasn't that easy. There are many wonderful things that can be done with hypnosis, but changing a personality instantly isn't one of them.

First of all, Dick had to learn what you have been learning as you read this book: *Locked within you are the powers that have existed in all the famous people of history*. You can't pluck an ability out of the air if you never had it, but you *can* bring it up from the inside, where it's been waiting to be used.

By using the pendulum, Dick learned that his lack of dominance was due to early training. His mother and father had over-trained him as a boy, had brought him up to be a "gentleman" and taught him manners and modesty at an early age. Of course there was nothing wrong with this—children must be trained—but Dick's subconscious learned the lesson too well.

In Dick's case, his other self decided that lack of confidence was the same as modesty. Throughout his formative years he never asserted himself—anytime he might have spoken up, his other self pulled him back and tried to make him invisible. By the time he became an adult, the conditioning was complete.

Dick was amazed as the pendulum produced this information that had been buried in his subconscious. But when he fully realized just what lay at the base of his problem, his job of re-conditioning became much easier.

Dick was taught to use his inner movie screen. *With a full, conscious knowledge of the re-conditioning process,* he began using it every night to see himself as a captain of industry, wielding vast powers with ease and decisiveness.

Of course, this form of daydreaming is not enough. The other self must be strongly impressed in order to alter its faulty conditioning, and nothing convinces like *belief.* Just to desire is not to achieve. To desire and *believe* is to achieve.

No matter what method is used for re-conditioning, it must be applied *with the expectation that it will succeed.* The subconscious will respond to nothing else as strongly as a firm belief that *this is the way it is going to be.*

Within a week of starting his treatment, Dick began noticing the change. Before this, when anyone asked his opinion he would beat around the bush or retreat, unwilling to "push" his ideas on others. Now he began to notice conflicts within himself, the birth of his new personality. When his old personality wanted to back away from the spotlight, his new self pushed him forward.

Dick forced himself to say what he felt, found himself using the word "I" more often. Soon he was enjoying the feeling of increased magnetism reflected in the attitudes of the people around him. When superiors praised him for his work, he no longer said, "It isn't much"—he agreed with them!

Within a month, executives who had never noticed Dick before were asking themselves why they'd overlooked his talents. A short time later he was promoted and is still climbing with the company.

This case is not an isolated one. You may have the same problem. If so, you're unaware of it—your other self is incapable of seeing that you need to change. You may not know how little you're getting from life. But you may be able to change your whole life if you don't already know that the way to more power is to believe—believe and achieve!

Points to Remember from Chapter XIV

1. All the great personalities in history possessed one thing in common—a belief in themselves.
2. The power to exercise authority over others is called charisma—it is not limited to the great.
3. Locked within everyone are the powers that have existed in all the famous people of history.
4. No matter what method is used to re-condition the other self, it must be applied with belief and the expectation that it will work.
5. You may never know what you are missing in life until you increase your personal power and see the difference.

Chapter XV

LONELINESS

There is a sadness about modern man, despite his achievements in the arts and sciences. In the midst of his vast communications networks, he is the loneliest of creatures, trying vainly to bridge the gap between one human soul and another.

It's ironic that this isolation should be self-inflicted, for each man is a jailer to himself, standing guard over his own impulse to reach out. There are a few who won't admit they need love—but even fewer who are willing to offer it before it's given. The result is a neurotic society where men and women wander by each other, crying out, "Love me!" as they pass but afraid to say, "I love you."

You may have seen the tragedy of men and women groping hungrily for an understanding that they won't allow themselves—cut off from any rich relationship by a childlike fear of being hurt.

Most people can't remember the moment when, as children, they first felt their love rejected. But there is such a moment for almost everyone, and children take it in different ways. In our tense and competitive society, a feeling of rejection in a sensitive child is likely to get plenty of reinforcement. So, as adults, their subconscious minds protect them by shutting off the ability to offer themselves—leaving them safe but alone, imprisoned by their minds.

How about you? Do you have trouble "connecting" with people. Do you wonder why you feel "lonely in a crowd"? Because your other self must justify everything it does, it builds up a philosophy to explain its withdrawal. In fact, it may even offer you a reward for your loneliness—a feeling of being "above" others. Have you ever thought, "I can't communicate because these people lack the ability to understand me?"

But a sense of being special won't compensate for long years trapped in the cell of your ego. *Don't cherish this kind of pain!* It may be precious to you—it may be your most personal possession—but until you put it aside, you'll never outgrow the child on the other side of your consciousness.

Your loneliness is a conditioned reflex. It may be strong because it's been growing for years, but it can be broken like any other habit.

Begin your breakthrough with yourself. When you go

to bed this evening, lie on your back and take deep, even breaths for a minute, drawing them into your abdomen. Now tense the muscles of your legs until they're rigid. Then relax them while you count to ten, until they're completely limp.

Follow this with the muscles of your torso, your arms and your neck. Don't forget your shoulders and keep up the deep breathing.

Every time you relax your muscles after tightening them, they'll be much more relaxed than they were when you started. Now you're beginning to feel warm, comfortable and loose—you have a feeling of drifting.

As you continue to breathe deeply, you feel yourself slipping slowly into a delicious, semi-conscious state. You are not really hypnotized, but, every time you exhale, you slide deeper into the borderland where your conscious mind meets with your other, hidden self.

Let your eyes close as you drift. Now you're face to face with your subconscious. In this condition you can speak directly to your hidden twin.

The world of your subconscious mind is a very strange place, where literal interpretations are the rule and time is an abstraction. To your other self, the past is *now* and anything you ever did is happening this instant!

Here, in the secret places of your being, decisions are made without your conscious knowledge or consent. If your father ever said you were bad, in this place you are still crushed by his judgment. If your childish love was ever rejected, here is the mechanism which keeps you from offering it again.

At this point, you can recondition yourself with any simple, powerful image forcefully projected. Remember, speak to your other self with *feeling* and *expectation*. Here's a case history which is typical of the type of problem and the type of treatment.

Doctors could find no physical cause for Ralph's periods of depression and self-doubt, but they were growing badly enough to worry him. Although he was a sensitive and intelligent man, he couldn't seem to get close to anyone, was unable to talk when he felt deeply about anything.

At times like these, Ralph felt a terrible sense of loneliness, as if he were "cut off from humanity." During some of these moods, he even considered suicide.

Ralph's problem was simply that he couldn't offer himself. Due to certain childhood experiences, he had come to believe subconsciously that his parents didn't love him. In defense, he had withdrawn into an invisible shell, hiding his fear and distrust of people under a surface appearance of gaiety and cleverness.

In adult life, long after he had consciously rationalized his fears of being hurt, Ralph's subconscious mind continued to "protect" him by keeping a wall between him and anyone who might reject his friendship. In fact, the more Ralph liked someone, the more his other self pulled away.

Ralph learned the principles of reconditioning easily. Every night he used the technique described in this chapter. Once he was in a state of semi-hypnosis, Ralph would say to himself, "The wall between myself and everyone else is breaking. I'm walking into the sunshine and I'll never go back to my loneliness. I can give friendship and love, and receive them."

While Ralph said this, he used his inner movie screen to project a strong image of himself breaking through the stone walls of a prison and stepping into a scene bright with sunshine and greenery.

After using this method for a little over a week, Ralph reported that he was having odd dreams. He experienced strange emotions, a feeling of lightness and joy that, he said, reminded him of his first puppy-love. Things *did* seem brighter and life seemed to grow more worthwhile. Emotionally, he was hurrying through various phases to become mature.

Ralph continued his reconditioning for several months, adding other suggestions to his nightly sessions as he thought of them. By that time he was, he said, a different man.

Ralph *is* a different man. He has never felt lonely again—in a crowd or alone—and his understanding makes him a valued friend.

Points to Remember from Chapter XV

1. In our society, most men and women want love but are unable to give it.
2. Many times, this is because of a childhood feeling of rejection that is allowed to become a habit.
3. Loneliness is a conditioned reflex—it can be broken like any other habit.
4. By using an image with feeling and expectation, you can erase your fear of being hurt and allow yourself to love.
5. The ability to give of yourself is a necessary ingredient of complete maturity.

Chapter XVI

SEX AND HAPPINESS

In the most primitive as well as the most sophisticated societies, men and women want the basics of life. These include food, shelter—and sexual satisfaction. The sexual drive is a very strong instinct. It's a factor in survival—built in, so that the human race will continue as a species. What better way to insure children than to make it a pleasure to start them?

Because the sexual act is pleasurable, the matter of children becomes secondary to sexual enjoyment. In certain South Pacific islands, the natives don't know that the act of sex is responsible for babies—they think women get pregnant because of the wind, or spirits, or several other things. On the other hand, sex is fun, so the birth rate is kept up even if they don't know why.

In our own civilization, we've gone in a full circle to the same point—having sex doesn't necessarily mean having children any more. Many of the old taboos about sex are gone, but their memory lingers on. Our society, advancing uncertainly toward a time when sexual freedom isn't necessarily sinful, is sadly confused.

This confusion, reflected in the childhood training of many of today's adults, is responsible for a great deal of unhappiness. The misconception that sex is sinful or dirty accounts for thousands of men and women who are unable to find fulfillment and are tormented by the thought that they're deficient in some way.

The most culturally enlightened and sophisticated people are often, subconsciously, the most crippled. Their other selves won't give up the lies they've learned as children and they can't admit consciously that they're influenced by a subconscious part of themselves.

Unable to face their own misconceptions, these people often convince themselves that a full sexual life is to be avoided. Having painted themselves into a mental corner, they insist they *like* it there and don't want to leave. At that point, any reconditioning involving self-hypnosis becomes pretty difficult.

Much more receptive are the people who realize they're being victimized by their own subconscious minds, even if they don't know how or why. One girl, Mary, was completely confused by her sudden sexual frigidity and consulted a hypno-therapist who was able to help her.

Mary and her husband had lived together for a few months before their marriage, and were entirely compatible sexually. However, as soon as they were married she found herself less responsive to her husband, and finally became totally frigid.

Mary was taught how to use the pendulum. With the therapist's guidance, she uncovered the rather common cause at the base of her trouble.

Mary's parents were rigidly "moral" people. When she was a child, they told her many times how sinful it was to have sexual relations outside the bonds of matrimony. Even then, they said, sex should be for the purpose of having children, not for pleasure.

After she left her parents' home and began living by herself, Mary met her husband-to-be and fell in love with him. Against all her childhood training, she began an affair with him and was surprised to find sex an enjoyable experience.

In Mary's subconscious mind, a pattern was established. Her other self "knew" that sex was sinful, and her relationship with the man she loved was given a secret, delightful flavor, sexually exciting in itself.

When Mary and her lover got married, their lovemaking was legalized—and her feeling of "sinfulness" disappeared. Since her subconscious said she couldn't have sexual enjoyment without sin, Mary became frigid—without the slightest notion of the cause.

Mary's case isn't unusual. *As long as people don't know what's going on in their own minds, their happiness is as uncertain as a stray breeze.* A short time after discovering the causes of her frigidity, Mary was able to experience normal sexual enjoyment.

There are other causes of frigidity. Some women have been conditioned to think of the sexual act as degrading, something just for a man's pleasure. Of course, a woman who feels this way is resentful—eventually, she rejects her basic femininity and her sexual drive. Frigidity becomes a weapon by which she tells her husband, "You can't satisfy me." But *she* is the victim of her revenge.

Impotence in a man is the equivalent of frigidity in a woman, but with a psychological difference. A frigid woman can conceal the fact from her husband, or even from herself. But when man is impotent, he knows it, the woman knows it, and he is likely to repeat his "failure" because it's been imprinted on his subconscious mind by a strong emotion—shame.

A man who fails to prove sexually adequate once can condition himself into impotence—especially if he's insecure to start with.

If a little boy is taught that sex is dirty and sinful, as a man he may be impotent with his wife because, subconsciously, he doesn't want to degrade her. If the childlike other self isn't brought under control, it will rule the life of the adult human being.

Another problem exists when a man subconsciously identifies his wife with his mother—and finds himself impotent when his other self keeps him from committing incest. Many men marry girls who remind them of "Mom" —which is all right as long as the subconscious knows where the similarity stops.

One businessman sought therapy for an interesting problem—he was entirely adequate with his wife but found himself impotent when he tried to commit adultery with his secretary. Obviously, his other self took his marriage vows more seriously than his conscious mind. In this case, he was advised to leave well enough alone and settle for his wife.

Except in cases where there is a physical factor involved, impotence or frigidity can always be handled easily, *once the problem is known and its causes are traced*. In the tangle of conflicting ideas in most subconscious minds, it's important though sometimes difficult, to locate the specific trouble. The pendulum or the inner movie screen can be invaluable in tracing these causes, after which any of the suggestive techniques described in this book can be used for reconditioning.

Sexual balance is important to the development of the complete human being. *Yours* can be achieved in the same way you achieve the total integration of your personality—with knowledge and application.

Points to Remember from Chapter XVI

1. Even in the most primitive or sophisticated societies, men and women need sexual satisfaction as much as food and shelter.
2. Our society is in a state of change—many things learned about sex in childhood have since been banished as lies, but the subconscious mind continues to believe them.
3. Frigidity and impotence are often caused by the other self working to uphold these cherished falsehoods.
4. Once the particular misconception causing the problem is traced and exposed, it can be erased by several different methods.
5. The achievement of sexual balance is an important step in the total maturity of any personality.

Chapter XVII

DON'T WASTE YOUR TIME—
Let Your Know-It-All Subconscious Do The Work

Every human being spends roughly a third of his life sleeping. Yet, no one knows exactly what sleep is, or what causes it, or why we need it. Men and women have spent their entire lives trying to discover why we must lie unconscious for several hours out of every twenty-four—and they have not yet come up with a theory that answers all the questions.

One thing we *do* know—sleep is very necessary to us all. Experiments in which volunteers were kept awake for several days at a time showed that after the first couple of days, the subjects began losing consciousness for short periods of time. These "lapses," as they are called, occurred three or four times an hour. Sometimes they would last for a couple of seconds, sometimes for a fraction of a second.

Most of the time, the subjects were unaware that they had caught a fleeting nap, but instruments showed that each time their eyes closed, the heartbeat slowed and the brain waves took on the characteristic pattern of sleep. Even if it's only for a second at a time, the mind must occasionally retreat across the border of consciousness.

In cases where even these "lapses" were denied the subjects, they soon became irritable, then lost their coordination and judgment. Eventually, some of them began to have hallucinations. Finally, several slipped into comas from which nothing could wake them until several hours later, when they came out of it refreshed—as if from sleep.

Scientists say that people who sleep deeply are more rested in a short time than those who sleep lightly, as if, with the subconscious more in control, the body can be restored faster. Certainly, the work of healing—both physical and mental—goes on much faster during sleep, and doctors always recommend as much sleep as possible for recuperating patients.

You may know someone who tends to fall asleep at odd times, even at a party or during a conversation. If there is no physical illness to account for this, it usually indicates a person trying to escape from psychological pressures. Sleep is a great gift—for a while. Unfortunately, we have to wake up eventually and face our problems, no matter how painful.

Some ancient cultures believed that in the world of sleep a man led a completely different life, and was an entirely different person. The few fleeting dreams they recalled on waking were, they thought, fragmentary memories of that other existence. As you can imagine, the dream world was a place of magic and mystery, where the dead walked and stones spoke.

Later, this belief gave way to the theory that dreams foretold the future, a popular idea then and now. Symbolism came into vogue, and those who could interpret signals from the other side of the mind became wealthy. If you'll recall the *Old Testament* story, when Joseph successfully interpreted Pharaoh's dreams, the grateful ruler made him a prince.

Later still, the "scientific" method had its day, and anything that couldn't be weighed or measured was declared nonexistent. Men of science found new theories for the wonders of sleep—and, certainly, these explanations were as good as any of the others.

Now, the pendulum is swinging back again. Recent experiments with extrasensory perception have shown that people can definitely receive the thoughts of others while asleep—these perceptions rise to the conscious mind in the form of dreams. So, once again, it looks as if our civilization will have to lean on the knowledge of a few thousand years ago.

But to those aware of the power within themselves, these "new" discoveries are not at all surprising. The subconscious never sleeps, and a dream is your other self's method of using the inner movie screen to give you a message.

Just as the healing process works better when you sleep, so does the creative process. History is full of famous men who learned how to let their other selves do the work while their conscious minds slept.

Thomas Edison developed some of his best inventions while sleeping. To his associates, it was a common sight to see the "old man" wander over to a cot and stretch out for a nap, to wake shortly with the answer to his problem.

Both Robert Louis Stevenson and Mark Twain, authors with entirely different styles, used this method for story ideas and dialogue. Stevenson would ask himself to develop a story just before he fell asleep—invariably, he would wake with what he wanted. He always said the "brownies" helped him. Twain claimed that in his sleep he could hear his characters talking—all he had to do was write down their conversation.

Abraham Lincoln often mentioned an inner voice which spoke to him late at night during the darkest hours of the Civil War. He followed its advice and believed it was instrumental in solving problems he could never have faced alone.

Depending on their backgrounds, people have drawn inspiration from their sleep in every field from engineering to poetry. These people learned how to release their subconscious minds while keeping direction and control.

Your other self is a storehouse of knowledge, but it needs guidance in order to serve you.

The next time you have a problem—in business or personal life—imprint it firmly in your mind as a question before going to sleep. Use one of the techniques described in this book and ask your other self to solve the problem for you.

Keep a pad and pencil by your bedside—at first, you may get the answer in one of those maddening dreams which vanish a few minutes after you wake up, so write it down immediately. But, if you continue this method for long, you'll soon be using your other self like a free consultation service. Also, the exercise will help break down the barriers between yourself and your subconscious.

If you're not using your sleep to get the right answers, you're wasting your time.

Points to Remember from Chapter XVII

1. Everything alive requires sleep in some form or another.
2. Since earliest times, sleep has been surrounded by legends, superstitions and conjectures—none of which could be proved.
3. Recently scientists have returned to an old belief—that in sleep the mind has powers not available in the conscious state.
4. Many famous men have told how they regularly received inspiration and answers to their problems in their sleep.
5. While your conscious mind sleeps, your other self can go on working for you—just let it know what to do.

Chapter XVIII

OLD AGE—
It's All In Your Mind

Recently, when a successful business executive turned fifty, his wife and children had a party for him, with friends and neighbors joining in to make the occasion a happy one. At one point in the evening, his wife turned to a friend and said, "Well, I've finally gotten Hal to say he's going to slow down. He's beginning to realize he can't keep up the pace he used to, even if he enjoys it."

The friend, who was acquainted with the powers of the subconscious, could only hope that she was wrong, that Hal did *not* believe it was time to give up the activities which made his life happy and interesting. Because—if he did—his life was really over.

One of the greatest mistakes anyone can make is to regard old age as something that irrevocably creeps toward you, bringing death with it, no matter how hard you fight. *Physical or mental old age can't touch you until you say, "I am ready, I am through—I quit!"* It doesn't sneak up on you—you call it!

Age isn't a matter of time—it's a matter of attitude. It is what occurs when an individual *orders* his own body and brain to "slow down." When you tell yourself every year, "I am a year older," you are urging your subconscious to tear apart your body.

In recent years, doctors have begun to worry about the number of people over sixty-five, both men and women, who retire from active life—and die. It seems obvious that the factors of aging and deterioration are speeded up when there's no sense of purpose, so the doctors usually recommend a hobby for a retiring patient and there has been a great increase in "Senior Citizen" clubs which promote social activities.

These are good steps, but they ignore the basic cause of the problem they try to solve: if men and women feel useless, no amount of planned activity can make them forget the futility of their lives. But—if you consider yourself valuable or feel the future holds interest for you personally, your mind will keep you young.

In a dozen different countries, men of science are busily proving that various drugs can delay the "aging process" in the human body. They've proven that people in their sixties and seventies can be rejuvenated, that the clock can be turned back even if the mind and body are far along the path to senility.

But what about the subconscious mind, which can control the individual cells of the body? In cases where extremely long-lived people could be studied, their bodies were found to contain the same chemical substances which are being used by doctors to retain youth. Your other self is capable of destroying you—or of keeping you youthful to the end of a long, long life.

Right now, your body is not old, or middle-aged, or even young. *It's no more than a few years old.* New cells are constantly replacing those that die. Even your bones can be considered brand-new every few years, since they consist of cells that have been created to replace those that are worn out.

Somewhere in your subconscious mind is a blueprint of yourself as a living being. Your subconscious sticks to this blueprint as it substitutes new cells for old. Without guidance, it will replace bones and tissue exactly as they are. This is why a broken bone or a scar will retain its deformed shape—as new cells are formed, they'll follow the pattern of what already exists.

With the proper guidance your other self will change the blueprint and make of you what you want. There are many, many cases of people who were told they were permanently crippled—or paralyzed—or scarred—who recovered and became better physical specimens than ever.

The subconscious can hasten, slow up or even reverse the process known as aging, and this can be dangerous for the individual who is unaware of the powers in his own mind. One successful and intelligent man applied for help to a hypnotherapist when it was almost too late. At the time of his first visit, Don looked like any hardworking businessman in his early sixties—energetic but tired. But that was the problem. Don was forty-one and completely worn out. He had no energy, his face was haggard and his body was that of an unhealthy sixty-year-old.

Don's doctor could find nothing physically wrong with him, but his mind and body were running down—heading toward premature senility, a disorder which can cause young people to die of old age—for reasons unknown to medical science.

To the therapist, though, the symptoms pointed to a subconscious cause. It seemed apparent that Don's other self was producing these symtoms. But in using the pendulum Don found that his other self was *not* punishing him—he seemed fairly free of the faulty conditioning which causes may psychosomatic illnesses. Then, as he talked about his background, a pattern became clear.

Don had started young in a business where age was valued more than youth, where gray hair inspired more confidence than youthful energy. In order to advance in his company, he assumed an air of dignity beyond his years. As he said, "I watched the older men at work—they were always more successful—and I imitated the way they acted and talked."

Don's strategy worked. He became successful, and this

SELF-HYPNOSIS 87

convinced him he was on the right track, so he became even more serious, more "elderly" in his actions.

The pendulum confirmed that Don's other self—*which he had instructed without realizing it*—had drawn up a new blueprint for his body and his conscious mind. If "old age" was desirable, it was giving him plenty of it! In fact, if he hadn't become alarmed by his symptoms another few years would have found him in a wheelchair, watching the active lives of men and women chronologically older than he but physically younger.

Although he claimed to be a poor hypnotic subject, Don soon learned the self-hypnotic techniques previously described in this book. As it happens in many cases, the *need* for help allowed him to succeed in self-hypnosis, since it was necessary for a cure.

Don was given an image calculated to do two things —reverse the aging process he had started and break the identification he'd formed that "old age" meant success and wealth. Every night, he would visualize the face of a clock on his inner movie screen. He would make the hands move backward, slowly at first and then more quickly until they were only a blur.

After about thirty seconds of this, Don projected a picture of himself, young and healthy. He found that photographs of himself taken a few years before were a great help in this, if he looked at them just before going to bed. After visualizing himself being active and youthful, Don would project the clock again. Then he would project an image of himself as a tremendously successful executive —the head of his company—but still young, vibrant.

At the same time, he began a mild program of physical exercise—not enough to put strain on his awakening body, but enough to gather up the slack in his muscles as they began to regain their tone.

In a month, Don reported that he was feeling much better physically and mentally. In fact, he felt so much more alert that he was making suggestions at work which met with favorable comment—they were the mark of a fresh, uncluttered mind. As his other self created a younger blueprint for him, Don's mind as well as his arteries grew more elastic.

The success of this treatment led to other experiments with men and women who were genuinely, chronologically older. After all, Don's "old age" was real—his other self had actually produced all the symptoms!

It now seems that given a stimulus the subconscious mind can be used to reverse the condition known as old age. As far as can be seen, even damage to the tissues can be repaired once the other self has a blueprint, a definite plan to work from.

There will come a time when senility is curable, as responsive to treatment as any other illness which is "all in the mind."

Points to Remember from Chapter XVIII

1. Creaky old age is more a matter of attitude than time.
2. The subconscious mind can control individual cells of the body.
3. The subconscious can destroy you or keep you young to the end of a long, long life.
4. Your other self carries a blueprint of your body which *you* can change to keep from "growing old."
5. When society as a whole realizes this, there will come a time when senility will be treated like any other illness.

Chapter XIX

PARAPSYCHOLOGY— TOMORROW'S GIFT

In spite of increasing evidence to the contrary, a large majority of American scientists still refuse to admit that the ancient powers credited to witches, wizards and saints are present in all of us. Yet, some are beginning to believe that extrasensory perception—the generalized name given to these powers—exists, and others are arousing public interest in parapsychology, the study of these same perceptions.

The disbelief with which our scientists greet the idea of extrasensory perception is understandable. Scientists and medical men are usually disturbed when confronted with facts that don't fit into cubbyholes, and extrasensory perception shows that our view of the universe may not be the real one, that on the other side of our physical senses there may be different worlds, with different rules of reality.

America, which has led the world in so many areas of discovery, is sadly behind the times when it comes to psychic research. For over forty years, Dr. J. B. Rhine and his wife, Louisa, have labored at Duke University in North Carolina, gathering evidence to prove the mere *existence* of extrasensory perception. On the whole, their work has been ignored by scientists in this country.

But in the Netherlands, Professor William Tenhaeff heads a Department of Parapsychology at the University of Utrecht, and in Russia the University of Leningrad sponsors research into extrasensory perception.

In general, Russia has kept ahead of us in psychic research. The Communist Bloc has never hesitated to investigate any avenue of knowledge which may have value as a weapon. Since a few of their successes have been publicized, though, America has been struggling to overcome its prejudice against the powers of the mind.

An example of our interest in extrasensory perception appeared in *Life Magazine,* June 12, 1964, in an article on dermo-optical perception, the power to "see" through the skin. The article documented the experiments of two Moscow scientists and their subject, Rosa Kuleshova.

Rosa can identify different colors with her fingertips—six inches in the air above the object she's testing! When she actually makes contact with a sheet of printed paper, she can read the print with her fingertips, or even her elbow, while blindfolded.

Sparked by the Russian experiments, American researchers began testing subjects for the same abilities. The first to report success was Dr. Richard P. Youtz, professor of psychology at New York's Barnard College. Dr. Youtz found that Mrs. Patricia Stanley, a housewife of Flint, Michigan, possessed the same powers.

Since then, experiments have continued in both countries. The Russians now believe that one out of six people in the world can be trained to "see" in this manner. If this is true, it's possible that some people who are now blind can be trained to "see" again—with their skin.

We are still in the infancy of psychic research, but a few things are obvious. There is no question that the source of all psychic power lies in the subconscious. Your other self controls a power vast enough to stagger the imagination—and the way to master that power is by breaking down the wall between you and your other self.

Almost every human being has some psychic power,

but most people have trained themselves to ignore the urgings of their own subconscious minds. They are afraid of ridicule—or of anything they can't understand. To an extent, learning to use your paranormal ability can be as simple as learning to listen to your own hunches.

How often have you walked into a strange house and had a "funny feeling" about the place—that there was a friendly atmosphere, or that something bad had happened there. Probably you laughed at yourself and did your best to ignore your feeling. Your other self, realizing you weren't interested, stopped giving you this kind of information.

But there are some who have learned to listen to themselves, to pay attention to the hints pushed through the barrier between the conscious and the subconscious. These people are the psychics, the paranormals who have a better view of reality than the rest of struggling mankind.

However, *uncontrolled* psychic powers can be very dangerous, as in the case of poltergeists. This is a word of German origin, which means "noisy ghosts." In the annals of psychic research, there are many stories of this phenomenon. In fact poltergeists are so common that a great deal has been learned about them.

When poltergeist activity takes place, objects move by themselves, often with no one near them. Teacups jump off shelves. Stones crash through windows. At one home, large rocks came bursting in. The house was in the middle of a flat field and anyone nearby would have been seen, but the stones seemingly appeared out of the air.

In some cases, heavy tables and chairs have been overturned. Houses have been virtually demolished when every piece of furniture "took off" at once and smashed into walls and ceilings. Often these phenomena include weird noises—groanings and moanings, the sound of animals, even explosions which are caused by nothing apparent.

Poltergeists seem to follow one family, or even one person, no matter where he or she may move. In the majority of cases, this person is a boy or girl just entering puberty. This fact has given rise to many theories.

At one time there was a popular belief that a poltergeist was actually a disembodied entity, a ghost, making a particular person miserable for reasons of its own. But poltergeists have been exorcised many times, without results.

Another, more modern theory has a psychological origin. The teen-aged years are full of emotional difficulties for most youngsters. As any parent knows, boys and girls in the process of growing up are full of conflicts and resentments, a boiling mass of newly-discovered emotions.

Usually the child feels a rebellion against authority—the parents—and guilt at feeling this way. Unable to express these feelings openly, the subconscious of the child projects these conflicts as a physical force—a poltergeist, which can destroy without being seen or punished, and for which the child can't be blamed. In a case like this, the conscious mind is completely unaware of the origin of these phenomena.

The motivating force seems to be strong emotion. Elsewhere in this book you've read that emotion and belief are the powers of your other self.

It's unfortunate that often the people who know most about paranormal power are the least well equipped to use it. They are scientists, and it's rarely that someone addicted to the scientific method has the faith necessary to set the subconscious mind working.

Slowly but surely, however, even the most hide-bound "realists" are beginning to realize that sometime in the future a force they can't weigh, measure or analyze is going to change the destiny of mankind. It is our destiny.

It is tomorrow's gift.

Points to Remember from Chapter XIX

1. Many of this country's scientists still refuse to believe in the existence of psychic powers.
2. In other parts of the world, however, serious research into the paranormal is being carried on.
3. At this point, it would seem that a large portion of humanity possesses "buried" paranormal abilities.
4. The evidence shows that a powerful emotion is one of the things which can trigger the power of the other self—and it is one of the methods this book recommends.
5. Even the most hidebound "realists" must come to realize that the study of paranormal ability is here to stay—and will eventually change the destiny of mankind.

Chapter XX

NOBODY LIKES A BULLY

Now you and your subconscious are a team, and you pack more personality into a single body than most of the people around you. To those who are still struggling against themselves, a really integrated human being seems to be a far happier, wiser person. At the very least, he seems to be more at ease. So, as you begin to develop your full mental abilities, you're going to find yourself feeling like the 98-pound weakling who became a bodybuilder.

Just as the body-building enthusiast slowly increases his physical strength through exercise, you've been increasing the power of your mind and will. Any professional athlete knows that real strength is achieved when the various muscles are developed evenly, rather than over-developed in some areas of the body and neglected in others. And by now you know that *your* power comes from an integrated mind, in which you and your other self work together.

You've been at your exercises long enough to show a change for the better—and inevitably, you will find that people gravitate toward your strength. In such a situation there's always a temptation to throw your psychic weight around, to use your power newly acquired like a toy. But if you've been reading the message that lies between the lines in this book, you won't.

The balance between your conscious and subconscious minds isn't going to maintain itself. *You* have to keep it in trim, just as an athlete must keep exercising to maintain himself at peak condition. And that means you and your subconscious must be in harmony.

If you like, you can bully others psychically. You can bend people to your will, push them in whatever direction you want. But you can't do that *and* keep your power, because you'll set up a negative conditioning stronger than anything you've worked to overcome. Once educated, your other self will set you free of false morality and useless fear. But you can't harm others and tell your subconscious that you're doing the right thing—not without inviting a lot of trouble.

This is where the power you're studying is different from other abilities. A businessman can be dishonest and still be a successful businessman; a surgeon's private life doesn't necessarily affect the skill of his fingers; an athlete can cheat and still be an excellent athlete. But if you betray the trust between yourself and your subconscious, you'll lose your power.

In Japan, where the arts of combat have been developed to an almost unbelievable degree, those who learn the techniques of karate are educated mentally as well as physically. Karate is part of the Zen philosophy, formulated by men who had fully mastered their minds. It was devised at a time when the Samurai—like medieval knights in Europe—held the Japanese peasants in slavery. And it made a weaponless man the equal of a man in armor, with a sword.

Karate demands both physical and mental discipline, but with it a master can perform feats that seem almost supernatural. Everyone has heard about the adepts who can break bricks with their bare hands, but there are other powers, less often mentioned, which show a command of the *whole* being.

Anyone can learn the techniques of karate, to a degree. But only those who pass a certain point are capable of *total* control, and these students are taught to master themselves before they're given the power to affect the world around them. In fact, the only way they *can* achieve the higher power is through a course of study that prevents them from using it badly. To use their particular kind of magic, they must be at peace with themselves— and a bully is never at peace.

Using your power to exploit another human being is black magic—whether you call it that or not—and those who do it are repaid in similar coin. Your other self knows the truth, and it's not likely to accept the glib excuses that your conscious mind uses to trick itself. In one way or another, there is retribution.

Several years ago we knew a young man named Larry, who had begun to study the secrets of the mind. In a search for Truth, Larry lived for a while in Korea with a monk who had spent much of his life in meditation. But

Larry lacked patience, and long before the monk found him ready to test his abilities, the young American had returned to the States, anxious to try his new knowledge.

Larry settled in Southern California and opened a television repair shop; he'd learned electronics in the Army. But he'd gone too far into the study of the mind to abandon it completely—and besides, he'd learned a few things he wanted to try out. He became involved with a group of people who met regularly to discuss Eastern philosophies and mental disciplines.

Because of his previous knowledge, Larry quickly dominated the group. Though they meant well, these people knew very little of the powers they studied, and Larry's experience made him their natural leader although he was younger than most of them. He began to enjoy the influence he held over them.

One member of the group was a shy but attractive girl named Vida. Just out of her teens, she'd been brought in by her father, who believed himself to be psychic and hoped that she shared his gift. At an age when most girls are enjoying life, Vida was deep in the study of psychic phenomena; she had no time for anything else.

Larry found Vida's admiration flattering, and told her he felt that she had great psychic possibilities, which would be enhanced if she would study under him. Her father, anxious to believe this, approved of Larry's interest in Vida. And Vida, who didn't have much choice in the matter, went along willingly with her father's wishes.

To anyone not blinded by his own self-importance it would have been obvious that Vida was emotionally immature—in fact, that she needed psychiatric help. But Larry's ego expanded pleasantly in the warmth of her attention, and he saw only that she was growing more and more dependent on him. Strangely enough, he wasn't after a casual affair, although he could have had that. He really loved her, and within a few months he married her.

SELF-HYPNOSIS

With the marriage, Vida's feeling for her father was transferred to Larry, who became a teacher/lover/father to her. Although the signs of her psychological imbalance grew more obvious every day, Larry continued to ignore them. He was too busy enjoying his domination of her.

Finally the inevitable happened, as Vida continued to deteriorate mentally. Reduced to a total dependence on Larry, and believing his stories of his psychic abilities, she began to think of him as a kind of godlike creature. One day while he was away at work, she neglected to run an errand for him—and rather than face his anger, she killed herself.

Larry has never really recovered. He's a lonely, bitter man whose home is like a prison to him, and whose life is a constant self-reproach. He knows now that the tragedy could have been avoided if his ethical sense had been as developed as his will.

It would be too simple to say that those who do evil will be punished for it—and besides, that isn't always true. But it *is* true that you can't misuse the techniques you've learned in this book without setting a powerful reaction into effect—either from within or outside yourself. Nobody likes a bully, not even the bully.

Points to Remember from Chapter XX

1. As you develop your mental abilities, you'll find that people around you tend to gravitate toward your strength.
2. You may be tempted to use your power to show off, to prove to yourself and others that you have it.
3. You can't hide what you're doing from your other self; it won't accept the excuses that satisfy your conscious mind.

4. If you use your power to harm another person, you are performing black magic.
5. No one can misuse the techniques of mental command without having to pay for it in some way.

Chapter XXI

THE MYSTERIES OF THE FUTURE

We have mentioned before that one of mankind's strongest motivations is fear—of pain, of death, of the unknown. Perhaps above all is a generalized fear of the future. The past is usually bearable, but the future holds all the terrifying possibilities that the mind of man can improvise.

For this reason divination—the art of foretelling the future, called precognition by modern psychics—has always been important as a supernatural undertaking. Whether one calls it witchcraft or ESP, anyone capable of accurately predicting coming events has always been in demand.

There are exceptions, of course. Cassandra, in ancient Troy, was supposedly cursed with the power of prophecy —cursed because no one would believe her, although her predictions always came true. As a final irony, she foretold the secret plan by which the Greeks were to conquer her city—and again, no one believed her.

However, the legend says that her plight was brought about by the god Apollo, who was angry when she refused to have sexual relations with him. If Cassandra were living now, she'd probably have a syndicated newspaper column; in the new era of insecurity, people are always anxious to hear the worst, no matter how they fear it.

Through the years, many different methods have been used in an effort to pull aside the veil of the future. Some, like astrology, are very precise. No matter who casts your horoscope, the results should be quite similar; the planets are fixed in their orbits, and their message is the same for all.

But for our purposes, let's consider the many forms of divination which rely on the diviner, the one who attempts to pull aside the veil. Some of these forms may seem very strange to us, for styles in fortune-telling vary like styles in everything else. The individual seer, if he uses an object outside himself to help with his prophecy, will naturally choose something in keeping with his culture.

People have interpreted the future in the entrails of animals, in the action of insects, by atmospheric conditions. There is a branch of divination called moleosophy which asserts that a man or woman's fate can be told by the placement of moles on the body. The course of the early Roman empire was sometimes swayed by the actions of sacred chickens, which were carried along to every battle so that their movements could be interpreted by the priests, and the battle directed accordingly.

Among some Arab tribes, to the present day, the key to the future is sought in the definition of lines scrawled in the sand. In Africa and in other countries where Voodoo is practiced, a much-valued object called a hand of glory is used. This is an actual mummified hand which is usually obtained from the corpse of a criminal, although it may have belonged to an ancestor honored for his wisdom.

Sometimes a candle made of corpse-fat is set in the palm of the hand, and answers to a question can be read in its flame. Or sometimes the hand is suspended on a string and an answer is interpreted from its movement, much as if it were a pendulum. In the case of a criminal's hand, the purpose is almost always negative—that is, for black magic.

The use of bodies or the calling up of ghosts for purposes of divination is called necromancy. It's an ancient way, very seldom used for good purpose. If you'll recall, King Saul is supposed to have gone to a witch who summoned up the ghost of the prophet Samuel, so that Saul could be advised on the eve of a great battle; he died in the battle.

Traditionally, ghosts have often been called up to help in finding buried treasure, on the theory that those who have been in the ground must know its secrets. But the dead, set free from time and space, are also believed to know the future. There are many methods—some of them quite grisly—by which various parts of bodies are used to solve tomorrow's puzzles.

With few exceptions, the most effective modes of divination are those in which the seer uses *himself* as an instrument, relying on outside factors only to the point at which they unleash his own power.

In ancient Greece, the oracle at Delphi was renowned throughout the world for the accuracy of its prophecies, though many of them were confusingly worded. Some of the confusion can be explained by clever showmanship, an effort to have the prediction turn out right no matter what happened. But it seems reasonable to assume that —at least in some cases—the unclear nature of the prophecies was due to the condition of the oracle's priestesses, who achieved their psychic states by breathing the fumes of a drug which was burned on the altar of the god.

There is no question that drugs can sometimes bring about a psychic state, "expand the consciousness." In Ethiopia, until the early twentieth century, use was made of psychic children who were called thief-catchers. These children, none over twelve, were drugged, then hypnotized, after which they could send out their minds and track down fugitives for the police.

But drugs carry their own risks, and the history of diviners who have increased their powers with such artificial aids is full of tragedies.

A safe but effective means of divination—and a way to test yourself for this psychic talent—is with a crystal ball. The origin of crystal-gazing is lost in prehistoric legend, but we know that any reflecting surface is useful in bringing about a hypnotic state; it seems likely that Dawn Man peered into a pool of water and was bemused by the visions he saw. Crystals appear in many legends, sometimes disguised as magic mirrors. In a later chapter we'll discuss their use.

Actually, a strong enough gift for prophecy will make itself known without external help, but there are cases in which a just-emerging gift can be detected with a crystal —or in which the subconscious has masked off the ability through fear. If this is so in your case, you should be able to overcome it.

Jeanne Dixon, the famous Washington seeress, first became aware of her power as a young child, when a gypsy fortune-teller read her palm and told her she would be a great mystic. The gypsy gave young Jeanne a crystal ball, and the child soon learned that the pictures she saw in it were real—or would be, in the future.

Although she still uses a crystal, Mrs. Dixon also sees the future in visions, which sometimes catch her unaware, although she can bring them about deliberately by touching a person or article. She is a Catholic, and what she sees in the vision, or in the crystal, is often shown through religious symbols which she interprets into a more everyday meaning. She has accurately foretold events of worldwide significance, as well as "reading" individual lives.

The outcome of her most important predictions still lies in the future, as she has foreseen a troubled time for humanity until the year 1999, when the world will be a much different place. She sees war in the 1980's, a global conflict which will kill millions before the citizens of a shattered Earth begin picking up the pieces.

With the year 2000, however, Mrs. Dixon sees a new society in which mankind, sadder but wiser, will finally achieve its destiny—and peace.

Jeanne Dixon's gift is a perfect example of how the subconscious can make itself known to you. Whether or not you have a psychic ability, your subconscious mind is constantly sending you messages, in symbols, which *must* be interpreted for your own well-being.

And if you *do* have the capacity for what our grandparents called "second sight", the only way you'll ever realize it is through the part of your mind which can penetrate the mysteries of the future.

Points to Remember from Chapter XXI

1. Most people fear the future, and many of humanity's magical arts are directed toward attempts to predict it.
2. In these attempts, experimenters have made use of everything from corpses to drugs, with varying degrees of success.
3. With few exceptions, the most effective ways to prophecy are those in which the information is allowed to come from the individual's own mind.
4. Using caution, there are ways in which you can test yourself for this ability.
5. If you *do* have this or any other psychic power it can only be discovered and developed through your other self.

Chapter XXII

THE MYSTERIES OF THE PAST

Someone once said that history is not written, it is re-written. Newly uncovered evidence is constantly forcing us to revise our beliefs about what happened just a few years ago. We've discovered that our own history books are inaccurate about events which took place a few hundred years ago—and anything farther back than that is a matter of guesswork.

Most historians, ancient or modern, are biased in their reporting; it's an unconscious attitude stemming from several causes. For instance, it's customary for the winning side in any war to re-write the causes and events of the action—and you can guess which side emerges as the hero. And then, there's a natural tendency for observers to be swayed by the emotion of the moment. Anyone who has ever talked to the witnesses of a traffic accident knows that there are usually as many versions as there were witnesses.

So it's not surprising that people are curious about the past as well as the future. The past is often full of surprises, even since the time—just a few thousand years ago—when men invented writing. Before that time, there were ages when civilizations rose and fell with no written record of their passing.

Scientists are slowly giving us a picture of the Earth—and humanity—as it once was. But this is a laborious process in which years may go by while isolated clues are drawn together and assembled into a design. And, as with traffic accidents, the evidence is open to interpretation. There are almost as many theories about Earth's early events as there are scientists interested in the matter.

Others have delved into the past in a variety of ways, using methods as strange—and sometimes barbaric—as those used to forecast the future. But it's easier to believe in the wonders of the future than those of the past. The past is supposed to be unchangeable, tucked safely away, and it's frightening to think that what we know about our origins is a thin membrane of guesswork, stretched tight over a yawning gulf of ignorance.

Despite this fear—or because of it—mystics as well as scientists have devoted themselves to a search through the maze of yesterday, working with psychic rather than physical tools. And there have been some whose minds were able to encompass both methods, both beliefs.

Carl Jung, founder of the science of analytical psychology, was a man whose studies of the mind led him into paths quite strange to his fellow doctors. He studied parapsychology, and alchemy, Zen and reincarnation, the myths of the past and the superstitions of the present. He believed in the existence of psychic powers, and he gradually developed a theory to explain the capabilities of the human mind.

Jung introduced the idea of a "collective unconscious", a vast pool of psychic awareness shared by the whole human race. This should be a reason why cultures on different sides of the Earth share the same legends, the same heroes, gods and devils. It could explain why present-day neuroses make themselves known in nightmares identical to those which troubled the sleep of our earliest forebears.

Jung died in 1961, and the full force of his discoveries has not yet been felt. But *he* was aware of their significance. "I am convinced," he wrote, "that the investigation of the psyche is the science of the future. It is the science we need most, for it is gradually becoming evident that the greatest danger to man is neither famine, nor earthquakes, nor microbes, nor cancer, but himself . . ."

From the idea of a collective unconscious, it's a short step to a theory of racial memory, which is supported by the latest biological experimentation. It's been found that a memory—not a physical characteristic but a *memory*—can be transmitted genetically by a substance in the body called RNA, short for Ribonucleic Acid.

So it's possible that every one of us holds within his cells the memory of the first mammal—or the first creature that crawled out of the ocean and became a land dweller. In fact, it's possible that indelibly stamped in our genes is the memory of the first life on Earth.

If, as the evidence suggests, there is a racial memory, we have to consider the possibility of reincarnation. If we have a memory that stretches back to the Beginning, it's believable that a single intellect, a spark which joins with the collective unconscious between lives, can survive as an individual—and remember past existences.

Edgar Cayce, a psychic who is better known now than when he died in 1945, believed in reincarnation, and his findings were seldom wrong.

Though he left school after the 6th grade, Cayce spent much of his life diagnosing illnesses and prescribing cures for them. In a trance, his knowledge was all-embracing, and his vision seemed unaffected by time or space. At various times he would prescribe a medicine fifty years out of date, or one so new that it hadn't yet been put on the market.

In spite of the fact that some of Cayce's remedies seemed ridiculous at the time, they never failed—and modern medicine is just discovering some of the principles he discussed in the early part of this century.

Cayce was a multi-talent, to whom the past and future

were both sources of the immense knowledge on which he drew. He described his own ability by saying he could connect with a Universal Mind which contained all knowledge. It sounds like Jung's collective unconscious, doesn't it? Or it could even be your other self . . .

Like Jeanne Dixon, Cayce was strongly religious as a child; he thought of becoming a minister, and his first inkling of his power came in the form of a religious vision. Also, like Jeanne Dixon, he prophesied a disaster enveloping the Earth before the year 2000.

But while Mrs. Dixon sees the catastrophe as political in nature, Cayce saw it geographically. He foretold a shifting of the planet's poles, causing earthquakes and volcanic eruptions, melting the polar ice caps and flooding the seaports of the world. He had seen something similar happen ages before . . .

Even when awake, Cayce had remarkable sensitivity. For instance, he was able to read people's emotions and states of mind through an aura which he said hovered around them. But it was in trance that he became free of any bonds—free, apparently, to roam through time and space without hindrance. And his view of the distant past was astonishing to those open-minded scientists who would listen.

Cayce's subconscious memory extended beyond recorded history to the continent of Atlantis, which he said finally vanished into the Atlantic Ocean about 12,000 years ago. There had been severe earthquakes before then, which had broken the continent into three islands; these eventually followed the rest into the sea.

In his trances Cayce described the culture and science of the lost continent. He spoke in detail of the instrument which powered most of their industry, an electronic device which sent invisible rays of light through crystal. His description came thirty years before the invention of the laser beam . . .

The destruction of Atlantis, said Cayce, came about

through a combination of accidents which caused this power to become uncontrolled. The breaking up of the continent occurred over a period of time; many of the inhabitants managed to escape to less civilized areas of the world. They carried the Atlantean culture to Egypt, Peru, Mexico, Central America—and in all these countries the pyramid developed as a structure of religious significance.

Cities in Asia Minor and Central America have names that are nearly identical; there was no apparent connection between these widely separated areas until a few hundred years ago—but the cities are far older than that. Cayce's description of Atlantean civilization was similar to the philosopher Plato's—but Cayce knew nothing of Plato.

Perhaps the most startling of Cayce's revelations about Atlantis was that its people are still with us; in fact, you may be one of them. Many of the souls that inhabited the doomed continent are living now in other bodies, he said. He firmly believed that the essence of a human being is born again and again—and that under the right circumstances a man or woman can remember past existences.

Cayce's powers were so extraordinary that his convictions can't be dismissed without careful thought. Like Jeanne Dixon, he often perceived his visions in symbolic form. But in a trance state, in touch with the "universal mind", his subconscious was quite practical and down-to-earth, as his medical advice testifies.

What if we *have* lived before? What if each of us has a treasurehouse of memories to call on and we could profit from past mistakes, learn from past successes? In our next chapter we'll investigate a method by which you can test yourself for this ability.

Points to Remember from Chapter XXII

1. The mysteries of the past, like those of the future, have always excited the curiosity of mankind.
2. According to the views of both scientists and mystics, our view of the past is not only incomplete but false.
3. Recent scientific discoveries have suggested that people have a "genetic memory", a cellular memory of the race of man.
4. There is some evidence that mankind also has a *psychic* memory of its past—and a possibility that reincarnation is a fact.
5. Each individual owes it to himself to experiment with this possibility, for those who are capable of piercing the veil of the past have a priceless gift.

Chapter XXIII

THE WORLD IN THE CRYSTAL

In every culture and in every age there have been those who knew that paranormal powers—the "magical" powers—rested in the subconscious and that they had to be brought to the surface in order to be used. We've seen some of the ways used to accomplish this. Among them are a few methods that must work well since they seem to have enjoyed enduring popularity with so many different societies. One of these requires a reflecting surface—any reflecting surface.

As we've mentioned, almost any shiny surface can be utilized as a self-hypnotic device, capable of stopping conscious interception of the subconscious powers. In societies where sophistication hasn't built barriers between the individual and his other self, self-induced trances are common. Used for a variety of reasons this form of self-hypnosis is often found surrounded by complicated magic rituals.

In ancient Egypt, priests poured ink into their cupped hands and searched out the advice of their gods in the black pool. In the South Sea islands natives dig a hole in the sand, fill it with water and look for visions in the clear surface.

In the Middle Ages, when it was fashionable for daring souls to dabble in the supernatural, magic mirrors were used, with appropriate appeals to the devil to summon up the images of the dead. A century ago, American Indians looked for pictures of the future in flat, shiny stones which they had "fed" by smearing them with fresh blood.

Rings, gems and candle flames have had their turn as tools for the serious psychic. It was only natural that with the invention of glass, crystal balls should become popular—and remain popular to the present day.

There is no "conventional" way to use a crystal ball, although fiction has accustomed us to the idea of colorfully-costumed gypsy-types making theatrical passes as they mumble spells over a clouded crystal. As with any other method for freeing the subconscious, the best way is, quite simply, the one that works best for you. Each psychic who has found this form of divination useful has, through trial and error, developed an individual style.

Very often, what you see in your crystal will be shown in symbolic form and must be interpreted, like the messages from your other self that come to you in dreams.

Even if you have a powerful gift, this is something you'll have to work out.

For instance, Jeanne Dixon has a very definite way of explaining what she sees. If she is reading a particular person, she uses his birthdate in order to find him in the crystal. The beginning of the year is at the front of the crystal, and she places the months that follow in their regular sequence; December is at the back of the ball, the point farthest from her.

Jeanne Dixon has learned to interpret distances in the same way, so she can tell if what she sees is nearby or on the other side of the world. In this way she can even tell when an event she sees will take place. However, some of these revelations are open to different explanations. Mrs. Dixon has said that her visions are invariably correct, but she can misinterpret the pictures in the crystal.

As you've seen in previous chapters, you don't need a crystal ball to free your other self. But if you think you may have psychic ability, this is one of the easier ways to test it—and it's fun.

First you need a crystal, which needn't be a "professional" crystal ball. These can be found in stores that carry stage magic supplies, but their price is usually exorbitant. You can do quite well with one of the glass globes sold in novelty shops, the kind that can be shaken to stir up an artificial snow storm. These are filled with water, which can be removed with the artificial snow. Re-filled with water, or any colored liquid, they make adequate crystal balls and will suffice at least until you decide whether or not you want to go to any more expense.

When you have your crystal, don't experiment with it until you can be completely quiet and undisturbed. Many psychics say that they find night to be the best time to use their powers. Some, like Jeanne Dixon, say that the hours before dawn offer the least interference from conflicting outside thoughts. But you may be able to use your crystal

SELF-HYPNOSIS

at any time—in the world of the paranormal, there are few hard rules.

Sit in a comfortable chair and place the crystal below and in front of you, on a table if you like. It's important for you to be at ease. Sometimes a light shining on the ball will help. Let yourself relax, and clear your mind of outside thoughts, using the methods discussed earlier in this book.

For the first time, at least, it's better to try for something particular rather than just trying to see what will happen. Picture someone you know who isn't near you at the time. Think strongly of that person and tell your other self plainly that you want to see what he or she is doing. Don't look *at* the crystal, look *into* it, and let your eyes go out of focus.

As you've seen in previous experiments with your subconscious, you may have to wait a while for results—and you may have to learn how to get the idea across to your other self. At first you just make sure that what you see is a genuine paranormal vision, not just a picture your other self supplies to keep you happy. That's one reason to start out by trying to "see" people whom you know—later you can check on your accuracy by consulting them.

Crystal-gazing can be fascinating—or dangerous. If you have a psychic gift, you'll soon be able to verify it. If you *don't* have it, you mustn't fall into the trap of guiding your life by false images. The deeper one gets into the study of the psychic, the more risk there is of straying into self-delusion.

We know of one case in which a life was almost ruined because a neurotic young woman with no knowledge of her own psychological problems looked into a crystal.

The girl—whom we'll call Lillian—had been visiting a therapist because of certain symptoms of hysteria. She'd often shown interest in a crystal ball the therapist kept on her desk, particularly after she'd been told how it was used by various mediums.

One day, when the therapist was called from the room, Lillian felt irresistibly drawn to the crystal. She had some idea of trying to see into the future. She looked into it and immediately saw a vision of herself being buried. It was an elaborate funeral; she saw her mother and father crying, her fiance mourning for her.

Becoming hysterical, Lillian rushed from the office before the therapist could return. At home she called her fiance and broke their engagement, then told her parents that she'd decided not to continue with her education. Since she knew she was going to die soon, she was going to go out and enjoy life.

Although Lillian's parents were disturbed by this decision, they might have gone along with it, but Lillian's insistence on her early death made them suspect she might have found out she was seriously ill. They contacted the therapist, who was as surprised as they at this new development.

At first Lillian refused to return to the therapist, but her parents finally told her she couldn't expect them to finance her "last fling" unless she returned to the therapist at least once more. At their next meeting she broke down and admitted what she had seen in the crystal.

To the therapist the vision—and the causes behind it —were obvious. Lillian was, like so many people, far less mature emotionally than physically. Full of self-pity at her last therapeutic session she'd been thinking "They'll be sorry when I'm gone."

When she'd looked into the crystal, her hysterical condition had made her extremely susceptible. And her subconscious had let her have her cake and eat it too, by letting her see herself dead and surrounded by the grief-stricken people who had not appreciated her when she was alive.

Simple as this explanation was to anyone who knew Lillian's background, Lillian herself found it hard to believe. Not for some time did she gain the stability to see

SELF-HYPNOSIS

horself objectively and recognize the vision in the crystal ball for what it was.

The therapist was badly shaken by this occurrence, which could have ended tragically. She immediately took steps to keep the crystal out of the reach of careless experimenters.

So go ahead and test yourself. See what the crystal can show you of the past, present, and future—but be on guard that reality does not slip through you fingers when you begin delving into the shadow world of the paranormal.

Points to Remember from Chapter XXIII

1. The use of reflecting surface has long been popular as a means of freeing the subconscious and its powers.
2. Those with psychic abilities have been able to achieve seemingly miraculous results with crystal balls, which they use to transcend time and space.
3. The techniques of using a crystal ball are simple, especially if one is accustomed to communicating with his other self.
4. For those who are immature, unprepared or unaccustomed to looking within themselves, there is a certain amount of danger in this or any other form of psychic experimentation.
5. Self-delusion and loss of one's sense of reality can follow if experiments are undertaken without caution.

Chapter XXIV

DARK PATHS AND HIDDEN PITFALLS

We've indicated that the study of parapsychology carries certain built-in dangers. The philosophies and exercises we've described can only do you good, insofar as they're designed to heal any mental wounds and evolve a whole human being rather than a mind at war with itself. But once you become aware of your potential, the urge to take risks with your new powers may seem almost irresistible. And there are things you should know before you venture into such uncharted territory.

It may seem that it would be wonderful to read minds, to know the future or to be aware of events happening far away. And of course it would be nice to have a power that set you apart, made you somebody special. But psychic ability can carry a large price tag—and, without abundant inner strength, being set apart can be a curse rather than a gift.

There is a high degree of neurosis among those sensitives whose ability came without their having sought it. Almost always, those who remain healthy under the strain are deeply religious, or think of themselves as keepers of a power that must be used exclusively for good. Often even these more well-adjusted sensitives are the victims of physical malfunctions that reflect great psychological strain.

Many sensitives seem childish and insecure. As children they exhibit the symptoms we discussed in Chapter XIX. Their psychic abilities may represent a protection against a world they feel is hostile toward them. Undoubtedly some, beset by visions they can't explain, drift into irrationality, and their powers never come to light.

For those who reach maturity and gain the knowledge to control their skills, there are other dangers. Exhaustion is one. The exercise of psychic power uses up a good deal of energy, and the possession of a paranormal ability doesn't automatically give one the strength to feed it.

Each paranormal gift carries its own risk. There are times when anybody would like to be able to read minds —but suppose one couldn't turn down the volume. What if you *had* to feel everyone's pain, frustration, grief? How long do you think you'd survive under such a load of anguish?

Or what if you could see the future but knew you were unable to change it? It takes a great deal of fortitude to see disaster coming and accept the fact that nothing you can do will alter it. Most seers find themselves unable to predict their own destinies, and parapsychologists are certain this is a subconscious defense mechanism. Life would be unbearable if, every day, we could see the next day's failures.

But most perilous of all, for both "natural" psychics and those who develop their ability through experiment, is the possibility of losing contact with the everyday world.

The structure of society is maintained by an unspoken mutual agreement amongst its members. Just as they work together physically to preserve its material condition, they form its psychic attitudes by a united, if subconscious, effort.

In a social sense, reality is pretty much what people agree it is. If you refuse to share society's picture of itself —and you must refuse, to develop your psi power—society will decide you've lost touch with reality. And that's an accepted definition of madness.

Even physically, it's been known for some years now that what we perceive as the world around us is far from reality. We can't comprehend the real nature of our universe because reality must be filtered through our imperfect senses, just as psychic visions are filtered through the mind of the seer with its welter of past and present neuroses. *No one* sees the naked truth.

Long study has revealed that one way in which sensitives differ from the rest of humanity is in their orientation. Our complicated society is word-oriented. Descriptive language is the basis of our civilization, and we even think in words rather than pictorially. But like many primitive peoples, psychics think in images, in pictures.

The natives of New Guinea have no words for colors; if something is blue, they say it's like the sky. The nature language of Tasmania had no words for tall or short, hard or soft; something slippery was like a fish, something round was like the moon. In an industrial technology, image-thinking societies can't compete with word-thinking societies.

The impressions of the true psychic usually come in pictures. His view of the world is graphic. An event in a vision may lie in the past, present or future, because the paranormal world lacks definition. So he must work out a code with his subconscious, heavily symbolic but allowing an exchange of information.

As you can imagine, in our society the paranormal often has difficulty in relating. Set apart in a culture that can't understand the way he thinks, he often retreats into a brooding isolation in which he can nurse his inferiority/superiority.

In a sense, those who consciously set out to develop their psi power are in much less danger than the "naturals"—especially if their efforts are applied through mental discipline. It *is* possible to live successfully in both

SELF-HYPNOSIS 117

worlds, but your path must be taken step by step—and with each step, your new knowledge must be united harmoniously with your present view of reality.

Sending your mind out to explore the unknown is perfectly all right, as long as you remember the way home.

As a rule, there are no results when psi is approached in a frivolous manner. Anyone knows this who has "played" with a Ouija board and gotten only nonsense for his pains. Remember, your other self is the guardian of all psychic phenomena, and it doesn't like to be taken lightly any more than you do.

But sometimes there *are* results. We recall a wealthy but rather foolish lady, a very proper socialite, who asked us to attend a "seance she was holding"; this was when the Bridey Murphy story was making headlines, and the lady had decided that reincarnation was "in".

As we'd expected, the "seance" proved to be a gathering of the lady's own crowd, people whom she dominated through her money and social standing. But, although the evening promised to be dull, we decided to wait and see what might happen. We were curious as to what she might provide in the way of paranormal entertainment.

We were introduced to an amateur hypnotist, an earnest young man, who was to officiate. After a few drinks and some meaningless conversation, the lady took charge and announced that she was about to be hypnotized. The young man would send her back to a previous life and she would entertain the guests with her adventures in the past, the implication being that she must have been Cleopatra, or at least Elizabeth I.

We settled back to be amused. We'd attended a number of these gatherings after the reincarnation craze set in, and we anticipated a spectacular failure. The other guests gradually quieted down, a little embarrassed by their participation in this meeting, more serious than their usual parties.

The hypnotist quickly put the lady into trance and

began taking her back through the years. He reached her infancy and pushed beyond, telling her to remember the existence before this one. And at that point the proceedings took an unexpected turn.

She sat up abruptly in her easy chair, opened her eyes and looked at the crowd as if she'd never seen any of them before. Then she leered at the young hypnotist and said in a broad Cockney accent, "Would yer like to 'ave a little fun, Duckie?"

It was ridiculous, a caricature of a London prostitute in a bad British movie, and for a moment the guests maintained a shocked silence. Then someone began to laugh, and in a moment everyone in the room was roaring. Her eyes blazing, the lady turned to them and spewed out some of the most revolting language we'd ever heard, still with a Cockney accent.

Completely undone, the hypnotist pushed her back in the chair and yelled at her to go back to sleep—which she did, abruptly normal though puzzled at the odd attitude of her guests, most of whom couldn't face her. Some were still trying to control their laughter.

Eventually, of course, she found out what had happened. To give her credit, she tried to carry on as ever, but she's never been quite the same—or quite as much a snob.

We still don't know if it was a genuine memory of a prior life, or if her subconscious had played her a dirty trick in return for a lifetime of false values. But, as you can see, it doesn't pay to play with psychic powers—at least, not with any preconceived ideas.

Points to Remember from Chapter XXIV

1. To those who are unprepared, the study of parapsychology carries certain dangers.

2. Many involuntary psychics—those whose power spontaneously came to them—are highly neurotic people, whose abilities came about as a defense against what they considered a hostile world.
3. For each branch of psychic endeavor there are particular pitfalls into which the unwary experimenter can sink.
4. Those who develop their psychic ability deliberately but without sufficient mental strength run the risk of losing touch with reality.
5. Sending your mind out to explore the unknown is perfectly all right—as long as you remember the way home.

Chapter XXV

THE VIOLENT INDIVIDUAL

No matter how good-humored you usually are, you've probably found yourself unable to control your temper from time to time. In fact, you may have surprised yourself by the manner in which you "flew off the handle" over something you later realized wasn't worth getting upset about. It's probable that, at least once in your life, you've recovered from a rage and been surprised by the murderous depths of your feeling.

We're told that in such especially violent times anyone could be understood for having lost his temper. But the truth of the matter is more complex than that—and its roots reach much deeper into fundamentals of human behavior.

There has never been a time when nations, tribes or individuals haven't been shaking their spears at each other, yet there are societies in which violence is virtually unknown, where kindness and brotherhood are the norm. They're few, of course, and far between. India, which preaches peace above all, is seldom free of rioting. China, which has the examples of The Buddha and Confucius to follow, has been the scene of numerous internal upheavals and is undergoing another at present.

Often the attitudes of a population can be discerned by an examination of its earliest gods—and almost universally one finds that the earliest gods are the bloodiest. These are the reflections of a people's childhood, they mirror infantile fears. Like most such fears they persist into a more worldly-wise age, impeding the development of true maturity.

Originally a disposition toward fighting was highly valued as a survival characteristic. Who could attract a woman without proof of his ability to protect her and his children from the dangers of environment? Peaceful types were eliminated as Nature strove to evolve a durable life form.

By the time family units began to develop into civilizations, feeling for violence also had evolved. Fighting became a matter of prestige, honor, revenge—a gentleman's sport. Wars were fought for land or slaves. Fear, instead of being a cause of war, became a weapon.

In the Tigris-Euphrates area of the Middle East, the first sophisticated cultures of our present era, understood the uses of fear very well. They were deliberately ruthless with conquered peoples. Their horrible reputations went before them, softening the fighting spirits of their enemies. Hills made of severed heads were left to mark the sites of destroyed cities so that the survivors would fear the very names of the conquerors. They did.

Social evolution changed the surface of things—but only the surface. In a way, the presence of written laws serves to reflect the warlike nature of man. Not that laws are bad; they're necessary and they prove that someone is trying to protect the weak and the honest. But their complexity proves that men have learned to exploit their neighbors in every conceivable way.

And, in the image of its makers, the Law has grown to be a separate entity in many cases, more interested in perpetuating itself than in fulfilling its purpose.

As this is written, there are few nations—large or small—that are not preparing for another major war even as they pray for peace. Weaponry has reached the point where only a madman would wish for war. But the governments of the world are stuck with their own conditioning, a negative conditioning that they can recognize but not revise.

As with nations, so with individuals. Struck by the increase of crimes against people and property, the U.S. government recently appointed a committee to study violence and its causes. The committee's decision, after a painstaking study, was that Americans are violent—and have been from the birth of the nation.

That makes sense, but it's incomplete. *Mankind* has been violent. And in any place where all the people are invariably gentle, either environment or authority has radically altered human psychology. There has never yet been a nation that, as a whole, has been able to change its hereditary combativeness into a more positive force.

But nations are made up of individuals, who constitute their "national" madness or sanity. You can't tell a nation to stop rioting, but *individuals* can learn to harness their destructive tendencies.

There is a deep reservoir of power in your anger, power which probably never has been used in a constructive way. Most of the time you smother your anger as soon as you feel it. Rage isn't nice; it isn't a civilized emotion—or so you were taught.

So when you're angry, you hoard your emotion and pour it into the little mental bottle where you've been keeping all the other anger. And when the bottle is full enough, it bursts—surprising both you and the object of your wrath. The current racial problem in America and other countries is partly the result of generations of bottled anger, held in for fear of reprisal until it had to explode from its container.

As an individual you can "work off" your daily load of irritation with exercise, cold showers, meditation. Or you can put it in your little bottle. Or you can turn the energy into something with more meaning and value.

The next time something makes you angry, put a memory-tag on it instead of trying to forget it. Later—perhaps before you go to sleep at night—take out that memory and look at it. Probably you'll begin to get angry again, but this time you can put your wrath where it will do the most good.

Everyone has ambitions that have been put aside for lack of energy, projects abandoned because of the work involved. Keep one of those ambitions in mind and, when you bring up your anger from your subconscious, *tell your other self where to place that vitality!* Get that anger out and make it work for you! Direct it against the purpose you've stopped thinking about, the plan you've forsaken—and watch your other self build a fire to ignite your ambition.

We didn't think up this method ourselves. We heard it from a man who had come to this country as an immigrant and worked as a laborer until he grew overwhelmingly angry at his daily ration of obscurity and shabby treatment. One night, as he lay awake wondering how he could stand another miserable day, something clicked in his mind.

He knew that raging at his bosses or his fellow workers

would achieve nothing, so he started to think about a construction device he'd been working on before he came to America. He hadn't seen it in use here, and he decided to build one in his spare time. He poured all his frustration and rage into his plan.

When this former immigrant told us his story, he was head of a large construction company. He still had plenty of day-to-day annoyances, but he considered them to be a business asset. He'd worked his re-channeling of energy into a regular system—and his wife told us he was the nicest man alive; she didn't see how he could do the work he did and never bring his troubles home.

A couple of years later we met a young author who had just about decided to abandon his career and go into some other line of work. Ignored and bitter, he was certain that his stories and articles would never be accepted. Almost jokingly we told him the immigrant's story, and the idea captured his imagination.

He decided to *direct* his bitterness, to turn it into a writing tool. Well, success came his way. He's still known as an Angry Young Man, but that's a designation that's become accepted—and he does very well at it, as well as having a place to put his aggressive feelings to constructive use.

Undisciplined anger, like anger bottled up, can only be negative. But it's a *force*, a *power*—one of the strongest —and it can be used to build a better life for you. Unleashed in the right direction, it can do more good for you and humanity than half-a-dozen "nicer" emotions. Besides, you can't get rid of it—so you might as well use it.

Points to Remember from Chapter XXV

1. No matter how good-natured you are, you've probably given way at times to uncontrollable anger.

2. History indicates that combativeness, no matter how unpleasant it may be, is a part of the heritage of mankind.
3. Individually and as a society, we're stuck with our anger; it can't be forgotten and it can't be tucked away without disastrous results.
4. But anger is a strong, vital force which can be re-directed into positive channels.
5. Unleashed in the right direction, your anger can do more good for you and humanity than your weaker but more socially acceptable emotions.

Chapter XXVI

THE GAP

Today a catchy phrase can circle the globe within a week, so it would be hard to find anyone who doesn't know what the Generation Gap is. Few other aspects of the contemporary scene have been discussed as widely as the current hostility between the young and the middle-aged. Although the gap is world-wide, there is in America, an aura of distrust that exists within individual families. It is not unlike a time of civil war in which fathers are pitted against sons.

To a degree this situation is older than the legend of Oedipus, who killed his father and married his mother. There has always been friction between the generations of males within a family, sometimes for reasons less simple

SELF-HYPNOSIS

than masculine rivalry or political intrigue—although history is full of deaths on both accounts.

The current bitterness between the generations is more complex but it is as basic as the drive for sex or power. Mothers and daughters enter into it too. Where it exists, the Gap represents a clash between opposing worlds, cultural opposites.

There is no argument harder to settle than one in which each party is devoutly certain of his own virtue. This feeling has provided the basis of most religious wars —and they're always the most bloody. Each side is for good and against evil—and each knows that it is the other side that is evil.

In the case of the Generation Gap, part of the problem is the old one of communication. A few days ago, watching a father and son angrily trying to get their messages across to each other, we were reminded of two young lovers we had once seen fighting. Their argument was over something completely insignificant, unworthy of such bitterness. But as we listened, we realized that the words had nothing to do with the quarrel. There was something that remained unsaid, and neither of them could bring himself to say it although it was the cause of the situation.

But, although it accounts for much of the world's troubles, lack of communication is a lesser cause of the Generation Gap. It's more as if two tribes from different sides of the Earth had suddenly been thrown together on a desert island.

In one tribe, each woman has many husbands. In the other, each man has many wives. After a day of watching each other, friendship would be impossible; there'd be bloody fighting because each tribe would *know* the others were perverts of the worst sort.

This kind of thinking requires no effort, no intelligence. In fact, intellect can't make a dent in it. An atheist and a devout believer can hammer away at each other all day without result. When you just *know* with all your heart that something is true, nothing is going to convince you otherwise.

Every culture has taboos that can't be violated without a sense of outrage. In Arab countries, a Bedouin would be forced by honor to kill an American who spoke to him as we've heard American businessmen talk to each other casually. The American in such a position wouldn't have a chance to defend himself—and it wouldn't matter if he did. The Arab would *know* a blow had been struck at his honor.

These attitudes are the result of conditioning, and as you've learned in this book, our society is no more free of conditioning than any other. But from inside the picture, it's almost impossible to see the frame around it—which is why we've devoted so much time to making that frame visible.

Our purpose is to make you free of non-thinking convictions so that you can rebuild your mind and spirit. Unless you've learned to recognize the picture you've been painted into—without your knowledge or consent—you'll never be able to really think for yourself.

In a rigidly structured society the older members have always governed, with appropriate dissatisfaction on the part of the young. Traditionally, the Establishment laughs off this discontent, knowing that by the time the youngsters are old enough to do anything about it they'll also be anxious to maintain the status quo. After all, would you want to change things when you're on top?

But the resentment has always been there—on both sides. The young look at the old and see the hated Authority figure, with all its restrictions. And, on the most basic level, the old look at the young and see the future—the future which will be alive when they are dead. Also, one must give up a certain amount of freedom to become "mature" in the Establishment sense—and the tamed animal always hates the wild one.

These circumstances have always been elemental, permanent—Established. But within the last two generations, times have changed radically. And part of the change was brought about by the same Elders who now mourn the passing of an era.

This age has exploited the young in many ways. When teen-agers were recognized as a consumer group, they were wooed by businessmen who competed for the new market with every psychological tactic they could bring to bear. New products were slanted toward the teen-aged buyer, and the Cult of the Young flourished.

Everyone likes to think he's an individual—different, special. Finding themselves lumped into a category in which they became individually invisible—like the Negroes—the young rebelled. They asserted themselves by speaking out when they had opinions, by investigating styles of clothing and hair which set them apart.

In an ironic, if unconscious, mimicry, the young began to see their elders as an anonymous mass—the enemy. "Don't trust anyone over thirty," they said, looking for strength in their solidarity as a group—a group the adults had created, had set apart from society as a whole in the first place.

The adults met this negative feedback with products of their own automatic conditioning—fear and anger. What right had these children to dictate to their elders? It was immoral! Worse—it was revolutionary! The adult psyche, prodded by the dictates of an alarmed and undisciplined subconscious, collectively responded with aggression. It decided to crack down. And it had the power.

Negative conditioning perpetuates itself. Violence begets violence. And a quality of youth is a lack of fear. This can be a strength as well as a weakness. The young have absorbed less of society's conditioning, they're not so ruled by the "Don't climb, you'll fall" crutch we spoke of in Chapter IV. Wars are planned by cautious old men but generally fought by headstrong youngsters.

So unfearing boys and girls went into battle with sticks and stones, and were met with the fury of a society that saw its taboos being broken, its pillars being torn down.

The battle lines were drawn, each side guided by a childish, uncontrolled and irresistible conditioning. The enemy was easy to recognize—love beads and long hair on one side; suits, white shirts and neckties on the other.

We know a couple in their twenties who recently drove across the country in a small bus. She wears beads, he has long hair and a beard. They are noncombatants in our Civil War; they both work but they both value their freedom.

On their arrival we received a letter. Sandwiched in between glowing accounts of the scenery along the way were descriptions of their continual "confrontations" with militant, middle-aged citizens. They were subject to abuse in towns that had never seen a "hippie" but knew well the face of the enemy, and they arrived on the East Coast bewildered by their encounters.

Humanity is altering. The emotional climate of mankind is changing, whether we like it or not. Young people are rushing toward the change, dissatisfied with the present and sure—perhaps foolishly—that any change will be for the better.

Rigidly structured older people are aware of the change also, but to them it seems like the onset of chaos—and those who support it seem tarred with the devil's brush.

The real enemy in the youth rebellion is neither the adults nor the teen-agers but a way of thought that afflicts both and is more suitable to apes than men. No one with an integrated mind could fail to see that this conflict is older than the current issues. Youth and age are playing out their ancient roles, but in an age too explosive for such games.

A war between the old and the young can never be won by the old; the young keep coming. And this time

SELF-HYPNOSIS 129

they won't automatically turn into conservative pillars of the community at some arbitrary age, because by that time the community also will have changed.

Never has it been so important to meet the future with minds free of preconceptions, unburdened by false conditioning. Our hopes for the future of mankind lie with the teen-agers of today, and many of them are coming of age with minds as constricted as those of their elders.

Only those in tune with themselves, liberated from the chains of incorrect conditioning, can break the negative feedback that is threatening society—and that means *you*, who have read this book and followed its exercises.

You have the techniques at your disposal to bridge the Gap, to break the bonds of anger/fear. Aware of yourself as an individual, you can accept the individuality of others—and spread sanity around you.

Use the magic you've learned! You've reconditioned yourself; now recondition those around you. You've discovered that you can affect those with whom you come in contact. You have a duty to the future to make the most of this, to open the minds of others.

Points to Remember from Chapter XXVI

1. The causes of the Generation Gap are not unique to this generation and are more complex than the issues involved.
2. The lack of communication is on a cultural, rather than a verbal level.
3. Both juveniles and adults have been reduced by this conflict to anonymous masses rather than individuals; to each, the other simply represents "the enemy."
4. Through a process of negative feedback, it has become impossible for those involved in the conflict to

escape it; they are conditioned *toward* anger, *against* reason.
5. Those who have learned how to master their own minds must use these techniques to help bring sanity to both sides of the controversy.

Chapter XXVII

TAKE FIVE...

A short time ago we asked a friend why he seemed so depressed. He grumbled, "The world is going to hell. My oldest boy wants to leave home. A new man at the office is after my job. And I can't meet my bills! Am I supposed to be laughing?"

As a matter of fact, it would have helped. Life is full of crises, but *they're not overwhelming if you meet them one by one*. Our friend had arrived at the point where he had so much on his mind that everything contributed to a shapeless cloud of worry hanging over his head.

This man is intelligent and sophisticated. Under ordinary circumstances he'd be capable of handling the problems connected with himself and not worrying about the others. He'd lost perspective because, for too long, he'd had no chance to get away from "heavy thinking."

Admittedly there are plenty of problems in the world today—in the previous chapters we've gone over quite a few of them. But it's possible to worry yourself to death without achieving anything. As a matter of fact, the more you worry, the less you achieve!

SELF-HYPNOSIS 131

Worry exerts a subtly paralyzing influence, making your purpose and energy drain away while you accomplish less and less. Finally nothing is left of the individual but a "worry wart," who lacks the power to be decisive.

As you know, the difference between positive and negative orientation is *balance*. Just as your conscious and subconscious minds must be in balance to make the most of your potential, both concentration and diversion must play a part in your life. If you worry enough about *anything* it can become an obsession, but that doesn't mean you'll be able to handle it well.

Your other self will work tirelessly on any chore you give it, but it's aware of your need for *conscious* diversion. After a while it will find ways to show you that you're becoming too single-minded, and it's up to you to understand the message. As Edgar Cayce said, "The mind and body are unified; one cannot suffer without the other following suit."

People have a tendency to get "hung up," to let some trivial preoccupation grow in importance until it overshadows things of real significance. At best this can lead to a joyless existence; at worst it can lead to neurosis, and by that time the subconscious may be doing its bit to make matters difficult for the individual.

An example of obsessive behavior is our society's preoccupation with physical possessions, to the exclusion of more important matters. We may soon be tested as a race, and our personal property won't sway the balance one way or another. It would be very sad if humanity died and there was no one around to throw all its possessions on the funeral pyre.

Once a stockbroker, whom we'll call David, came to us for help with his memory, which had been growing worse for some time. By the time he asked us to hypnotize him, David was aware that he had a real problem. He had no trouble with dates, names or places, but he was constantly forgetting personal possessions.

Wherever he went, David left behind him a trail of sunglasses, cigarette lighters, appointment books, etc. His forgetfulness was becoming obvious to others. Since they might think that this condition affected his work, he was worried about losing some of his valuable accounts—and it seemed that the more he worried, the more things he happened to forget.

One of David's friends, an amateur psychologist, suggested several Freudian explanations for his behavior, but David considered himself a hard-headed realist—none of that analytical stuff for him! In fact, he was stretching his principles a bit by going to a hypnotist.

But he considered his problem a simple one, and came to us as he would have gone to a plumber if his kitchen sink had been stopped up. It was just a matter of unclogging his memory, and he asked us to fix it as soon as possible so that he could get back to business. Naturally, the problem proved to be a little more complicated than David had expected.

It developed that David's subconscious was trying to make itself heard in the most obvious possible way. David had been born poor; his success as a stockbroker had been achieved through hard work, and he was justifiably proud of himself. But, especially in recent years, material success had come to mean more and more to him.

With the acquisition of a large house, an expensive car and the other trappings of success, David worked harder than ever rather than allowing himself to relax; he was determined never to fall back into poverty. He couldn't admit it, but fear was at the bottom of all his effort. He didn't really think he deserved his prosperity, and suspected that some day he would lose it all.

In this way David established a conditioning which permitted him no pleasure except in the accumulation of more property, more possessions. Eventually his imbalance began to make itself known in small ways, but he had never paid much attention to hunches from his subconscious—except if they applied to stocks and bonds.

So his other self finally took drastic action in an effort to drop some of the possessions that were, indeed, "clogging" him; it saw to it that he simply left them behind, wherever he went.

As you can imagine, it was hard to make David see what was going on—and it was necessary to do this before we could accomplish anything to connect his "memory" lapses. But eventually—with common sense playing as large a part as anything we said—he broke through this conditioning. There's been nothing wrong with his memory since he learned to relax a little. And he's not afraid to any more, either.

This case is typical of the ease with which one can fall into an unhealthy unbalanced state. We're not saying that David should have given away his hard-earned money or turned his back on the career in which he had been successful. But no one can concentrate on one facet of life, to the exclusion of everything else, and remain healthy.

There's no problem in the world so important that you can't take time out to refresh your mind—and return to the problem in better shape. We live in a hard-driving, success-oriented world—and it's full of men and women who drink too much, who have ulcers, who wake up tired and greet each day with dread.

Success, like everything else, is relative. It's nice to have money, but—believe it or not—all the money in the world won't make you happy if you've become too neurotic to enjoy friendship and relaxation.

We've never met a person who managed to achieve both success and happiness without mastering an important quality—the ability to *stop thinking*. Everyone realizes how important rest is to the body, but few are aware of how important it is for the *mind* to rest.

Even if your other self is busily working for you, your *conscious mind* must be allowed to go into neutral now and then. Those who can successfully face today's problems have learned this truth, whether or not they've learned to free their other selves. And those who *do* learn to communicate with their subconscious minds are soon aware that this kind of rest is necessary to physical and mental well-being.

Name your ambition. Whether it's love or money, you can't devote yourself to it totally without losing your health—and, once it's gone, you can't buy health for love or money.

You may have ignored or neglected your needs in this area, but your pendulum will tell you how important it is to "turn off" your mind from time to time. When next you feel tired, listless, run-down—all the cliches of the advertising world—ask your other self if you shouldn't have a few minutes of conscious rest, and you may be surprised at how quickly the pendulum will respond.

This kind of fatigue is like a vitamin deficiency. It creeps up so gradually that the individual is unaware of his condition until, suddenly, life seems colorless and flat. Day-to-day living becomes a chore, and the mind is incapable of consciously recognizing its own symptoms.

But the subconscious is aware, and the cure is as simple as taking a vitamin pill. It could be a change of scenery, or a good laugh, or simply getting involved in something else for a while. But if that's impossible, you have the techniques at your disposal to give yourself that "vitamin pill" right where you are.

All you need is a quiet place where you can sit or lie down comfortably. Close your eyes and contact your other self—by now this should be as easy as making a telephone call. Explain that you want to give your conscious mind a rest, that you want to "take five"—and relax, using the method described in Chapter II.

You won't fall asleep, but you'll experience a rapid transition into the state where you will "drift." That is, your conscious mind will busy itself with surface prob-

SELF-HYPNOSIS 135

lems for just a few seconds and then your other self will take over.

If you like, you can even take a trip through some pleasant experience in your past; the important thing is to let go and float with the mental tide. Within a few minutes you can resume your normal activities, and you'll feel as if you've slept for a week! Your other self has just been waiting for the opportunity to rejuvenate you.

We know an enterprising businessman who follows this routine once a day. Wherever he is—and he travels a good deal—he manages to find a quiet spot where he can let go. Through practice he can just lean back, say to himself, "Take five!" and his subconscious does the rest. His friends marvel at his vitality.

Sometimes it's possible to forget your earliest, simplest exercises, just because you've gone far beyond them into more interesting projects. But the procedures you learned at the beginning of this book are still the most effective for keeping you and yourself working well together. If you use them regularly you'll go on to your ultimate goal in safety. If you don't, you'll waste valuable time and energy on an uphill climb.

Points to Remember from Chapter XXVII

1. Troubles will not be overwhelming if they're handled one by one.
2. Unproductive worry makes you *less* able to handle your problems.
3. Your *conscious mind* needs to be diverted from constant attention to one subject, which can result in obsessive behavior.
4. You can give yourself the needed "break" from your problems by using one of the simple exercises you've learned in this book.

5. No matter how greatly you develop your capacities, those early lessons will still be necessary and valuable.

Chapter XXVIII

RITE OF PASSAGE

All societies recognize that there are important points in a person's life that mark a transition from one status to another—birth, naming, coming of age, marriage, death. In primitive groups these are usually marked by rituals intended to ease the way, for everyone knows that each step in the life cycle is perilous.

Anthropologists call these rituals, "rites of passage." We believe that humanity is presently in need of such a rite. The human race is coming of age, and it would be comforting if some cosmic witch-doctor could assure us that the years ahead will be safe, marking an easy passage rather than a decline into insanity or death.

It would be of some cheer to feel that the world's present instability is a minor matter of adjustment, like an adolescent's pimples, or like painful but temporary "growing pains." But it reminds us more of a movie we once saw in which two men grappled in a small boat, too engrossed in their struggle to realize that the current was carrying them toward rapids that would kill them both.

Only the stubbornly unrealistic can fail to realize that humanity is heading toward change. Neither fear nor bravado will see us through, only understanding and a willingness to give up childish things. There is need of a New Way of thinking. We believe that the procedures we've outlined in this book point to that way.

We've talked quite a bit about the need to break your conditioning, to destroy your present point of view. A friend who has read the manuscript of this book says that we're recommending anarchy, but this isn't the case. We have no interest in tearing down society. Society is tearing itself down. We have an interest in survival—as we think you do. We are trying to give you a handbook in survival.

The potential of mankind is far from fulfilled, there's been quite a lag between our ambitions and our achievements. But the difference between the dream and the fact is what drives man forward. Only the future can tell whether it drives us upward or downward.

The next thirty or so years will be fascinating, as will the aftermath of whatever upheaval awaits us. We have a vision of a world transformed by the power of the mind. Perhaps man's psychic powers will finally be brought into play. If there are still psychiatrists, they may be able to read their patients' minds; doctors may be able to heal through mental energy.

On the other hand, wars may be fought by people directing evil thoughts against the enemy, destroying men and machines at long range. Each time humanity develops another talent, it's like a scientist experimenting with a new germ culture; it may cure something if he looks around long enough, or it may kill him.

An unlimited war could drive us back to savagery. A few thousand years from now, scholars may be debating whether there ever was an ancient continent called America that vanished into the sea in a giant cataclysm. Or people from outer space, tourists from the stars, may come in excursion vessels to view the remains of Earth, cindered by its own stupidity.

Whatever happens, we've come to believe that whoever is alive now will be there. Each man bears humanity in his genes; some part of each of us will be around again, living in some future member of the race.

Will boredom still be one of humanity's problems? Will fear be gone or will the great unknown still have its old effect? When people ride between the stars, will loneliness still take its toll on minds that need the warmth of other minds? Now is a good time to be alive—but tomorrow will be better.

In the meantime, let's not forget to make the most of the present. Despite its attractiveness, dreaming of tomorrow offers only a temporary reprieve from the troubles of today. And don't forget—you have a responsibility to today.

If this book has helped you know your other self, it has served its purpose—but you have yet to serve yours. If you've gained strength, you are a rock in a sea of weakness. But remember, no man is an island. As near to you as the next human being, someone may be drowning in fear.

As you become more sensitive to your other self and the miracle which is your integrated mind, you'll find yourself more perceptive in ways that may be unsettling. But there is a line between reaching out to touch the minds of others and getting caught up in them. Your strength will continue to grow.

We haven't said all there is to say, but you have to go on by yourself. You'll find your own new questions—and the answers to them.

In closing we can do no better than to quote from an anonymous philosopher who said, in 1692, "Go placidly amid the noise and haste, and remember what peace there may be in silence. As far as possible without surrender be on good terms with all persons. Speak your truth quietly and clearly and listen to others, even the dull and ignorant; they too have their story.

"Keep interested in your own career, however humble; it is a real possession in the changing fortunes of time. Exercise caution . . . for the world is full of trickery. But let this not blind you to what virtue there is; many persons strive for high ideals, and everywhere life is full of heroism.

"Be yourself. Especially, do not feign affection. Neither be not cynical about love; for in the face of all aridity and disenchantment it is as perennial as the grass.

"Nurture strength of spirit to shield you in sudden misfortune. But do not distress yourself with imaginings. Many fears are born of fatigue and loneliness. Beyond a wholesome discipline, be gentle with yourself.

"You are a child of the universe no less than the trees and the stars; you have a right to be here. And whether or not it is clear to you, no doubt the universe is unfolding as it should.

"Therefore be at peace with God, whatever you conceive him to be . . . and in the noisy confusion of life keep peace with your soul. With all its sham, drudgery and broken dreams, it is still a beautiful world. Be careful. Strive to be happy . . ."

SAVE MONEY . . . TAKE ADVANTAGE OF OUR SPECIAL PRICE OFFER!

Order 1 book —Pay only 60¢, plus 10¢ for postage and handling.

Order 2 books—Pay only $1.00—We pay postage.

Order 4 books—Pay only $2.00—We pay postage.

Order 6 books—Pay only $3.00—We pay postage.

Discounts up to 47%—If purchased on newsstands, books on this list will cost from 60¢ to 95¢ each. Now—regardless of cost—all at one low, low price!

KINGDOM OF DREAMS
J. & P. Schuyler

Why you dream . . . what your dreams mean . . . how they affect your present and future life. Learn to tune in to the power of the unconscious. **A389**

7 WAYS TO TELL FORTUNES AND PREDICT THE FUTURE
Jodra Petrie

Explained are: the Tarot, numerology, cup tossing, astrology, card reading, palmistry, and spirit spelling. With step-by-step instructions for using each system. **A388**

The most definitive, up-to-date report on psychic research into the world of the dead—*with startling case histories of spirit communication!*

VOICES FROM BEYOND

Brad Steiger

True incidents that prove life beyond death

A381

What was the frightening truth about a centuries-old curse that threatened a beautiful young woman?

THE UNDYING MONSTER
by Jessie Douglas Kerruish

For a thousand years the Hammond family had been at the mercy of a fiendish monster. When it attacked Oliver Hammond, the villagers were not surprised. But for Oliver's sister, Swan Hammond, the tragedy meant horror as well as sorrow—for she knew she would be the next victim of this creature from hell!

A351

ESP, YOUR SIXTH SENSE — Brad Steiger
Do you have extrasensory perception? Does everyone? Is there such a thing as telepathy? Can anyone really see or predict the future? Find out in this amazing book.
A205

THIS IS SPIRITUALISM — Maurice Barnabell
Whether you believe in life after death or not, this is a tremendously provocative book.
A288

THE POWER OF HEALING — Harry Edwards
An inspiring book by a man with the miraculous gift of curing the sick. It presents the healing story in a simple way, to show how all who are in need of it can benefit from it.
A305

SAVE MONEY ... TAKE ADVANTAGE OF OUR SPECIAL PRICE OFFER!

Award books retail at prices from 60¢ to 95¢ per title wherever paperbound books are sold. You may order any of these books directly from us at special reduced prices. Use the special order coupon on the last page.

Absorbing, informative, brimming with astonishing case histories ...

THE ABOMINABLE SNOWMEN

Eric Norman

Proof that these incredible creatures exist in well populated areas of the United States ... authenticated eyewitness accounts of nature's weirdest phenomenon. This book may well be the most thorough study on the incredible Abominable Snowmen.

A479

WITCH HOUSE — Evangeline Walton
An Award novel of Gothic horror—An innocent young girl is trapped in a house of evil ... chosen against her will to serve the dark lord of hell. **A481**

HOW HANDWRITING ANALYSIS CAN IMPROVE YOUR LIFE — Robert Holder
Use graphology to reveal: personality, intellect, creativity, hidden illness, emotional stability, sexual prowess, and much, much more. **A445**

FLYING SAUCERS ARE HOSTILE — Brad Steiger & Joan Whritenour
UFO atrocities, from strange disappearances to bizarre deaths. The evidence set forth is terrifying—and true! You dare not allow yourself to ignore it. **A234**

WITCHES AND THEIR CRAFT — Ronald Seth
A complete and unexpurgated account of witchcraft—from earliest rites to the "Rosemary's Baby" practices of today. **A472**

REAL GHOSTS, RESTLESS SPIRITS AND HAUNTED MINDS
Brad Steiger

True, documented encounters with the supernatural! Forget about strange phantoms in bed sheets or stray wisps of misty ectoplasm. This is a book about real ghosts—and why and where and how they do their haunting!
A299

HYPNOSIS
H. D. Birns

Hypnosis can show you how to make more money; achieve full sexual satisfaction; eliminate anxiety and fears; get along better with everyone; never feel tired again; lose weight, control drinking, stop smoking—and much more. Learn the amazing technique of self-hypnosis.
A298

BID BETTER, PLAY BETTER
Dorothy Hayden

Unique book that will increase your skill and enjoyment of bridge. A243

CONJURE WIFE

by Fritz Leiber

A modern classic of terror and suspense

Does witchcraft still flourish today? Can an ordinary young woman practice sorcery?

He asked himself these questions as he watched his wife with growing terror . . . as he stood helplessly by, seeing the dark shadows of evil trap her in a web of witchcraft!

"Leiber has never written anything better."
A341

"In Gurdjieff, the ancient teachings of Lao Tse, Jesus and St. Augustine all have fresh import."

—Frank Lloyd Wright

A STUDY OF GURDJIEFF'S TEACHING
Kenneth Walker

Gurdjieff challenges each of us to find the answers to the deepest questions man can ask about himself and the universe. A remarkable book revealing the wisdom of a master who shows the way to a new world of understanding and self-knowledge.

A468

SAVE MONEY . . . TAKE ADVANTAGE OF OUR SPECIAL PRICE OFFER!

Order 1 book —Pay only 60¢, plus 10¢ for postage and handling.
Order 2 books—Pay only $1.00—We pay postage.
Order 4 books—Pay only $2.00—We pay postage.
Order 6 books—Pay only $3.00—We pay postage.

AWARD BOOKS, P. O. Box 2080, Dept. A501
Grand Central Station, New York, N. Y. 10017

Please send me the books marked below:

A205	A288	A305	A381	A445	A479
A234	A298	A341	A388	A468	A481
A243	A299	A351	A389	A472	

If any of my selections are out of stock, please supply the following alternate choices:

Name_____

Address_____

City_____ State_____ Zip Code_____

Send remittance in U. S. or Canadian funds. Sorry no C.O.D.'s.
We pay postage and handling on all orders of $1.00 or more.